A Guide to Pagan Camping

Other works by Lori Dake are available online via:

- **The Pagan Newswire Collective**:
(www.PaganNewswireCollective.com)

- **The Witches' Voice**: www.Witchvox.com

- **Suite 101**: www.Suite101.com

and many more!

A Guide to Pagan Camping

Festival Tips, Tricks and Trappings

Lori Dake

ROTCO MEDIA

Rotting Corpse Records - Media Division

www.rottingcorpserecords.com

ROTCO MEDIA books are published by:

Rotting Corpse Records – Media Division

PO Box 306

Chicago, IL 60690-0306

United States of America

A Guide to Pagan Camping: Festival Tips, Tricks and Trappings

Copyright © 2011 by Lori Dake

Cover illustration and interior layout by Lori Dake

Cover layout by Ron Dake

All rights reserved. No part of this book may be reproduced or transmitted in any form or by any means without express written permission of the author.

ISBN-13: 978-0615456270
ISBN-10: 0615456278

For my handsome fellas

Acknowledgments

I want to thank my family and friends who have offered me a great deal of advice with the production and publishing of this book. That goes as well for all the online folks who've been viewing my site over the years. If it wasn't for you all, I would have no audience.

I also would like to thank Edward Murphy and the Law named for him. If it wasn't for that law stirring up problems, I would have no failures to learn from.

Blessings!

Table of Contents

PART I – All About the Fest

The Not-So-Inclusive Festival List 5
The Pagan Camping Checklist 7
Checklist Details 11
Food, Clothing and Shelter 15
The (Not So) Hidden Costs of Pagan Festivals 37
Packing Up and Heading Out 43
Festival Dos and Don'ts 51
Arriving at the Fest! 57
Camp Kitchen Preparation 63
Dressing Up Your Pagan Campsite 77
Playing Nice in the Sandbox 83
Building Community Through Your Gifts and Talents 91
When the Fest is Over 117

Part II - My Fool-Proof Pre-/Camping Recipes

Sample Menu 123
Breakfasts 143
Lunches 151
Dinners 163
Desserts 179
Potlucks 185

Welcome and Well Met!

> *"Why aren't we flying? Because getting there is half the fun. You know that."*
> —Clark Griswold, *National Lampoon's Vacation*

Hey there Festie and welcome to my literary abode! Pour yourself a tall glass of something cool and hunker down for some serious highlighting and bookmarking. By the time you finish reading, I'm sure you're going to be digging through your camping supplies itching to head out on the open road.

In case you picked this up by mistake, this book is all about Neo-Pagan camping, primarily focused on festivals and gatherings. From my experiences at various fests, and at various public campgrounds over the years, I felt safe enough to take my somewhat meandering online articles to the next level by merging them into structured book form. I figured since a website can easily disappear, and because it can be rather hard to read an online article out in the woods, I should go ahead and put the articles all together, just so people like you have something tangible to bring with you where you would need the information most.

Since I was a baby, my mom and dad used to take us on these two week to month-long, cross-country excursions every summer, on an extremely tight budget no less. (One trip was in fact eerily similar to that famous road trip movie everyone knows and loves - lost luggage, car breakdown and all.)

On the first day of our journey, Dad would wake us all up at four in the morning in order to beat traffic out of the city. After we adjusted to being awake, my brother and I would drive him nuts with our repetitious and monotonous games in the back seat for several hours. Between driving a good three hundred miles a day, we would stop for a simple breakfast and lunch at rest stops, eating out of a metal cooler. (I seem to recall a snowman on the front of that cooler.) After several hours and perhaps cutting through more than one state, we would finally arrive at a camp ground. Each afternoon involved setting up camp, and each evening included making dinner over the fire - in all kinds of weather. Some nights, Dad would be too tired to cook, so we would have a pizza delivered to us, or we'd drive into town for a burger. The following morning, we'd eat breakfast out of the cooler again, pack everything up and drive for several hours once more to the next camping destination.

For the most part, our vacations were pretty self-reliant without many conveniences or luxuries, unless one considers rusty boat-mobiles luxuries. (Dad sure did like his oldschool luxury sedans.) It is from those experiences, as well as the ones I gained at fests (which are the same yet very different), I would like to believe they really should be shared with fine folks like you. That way, you can benefit from my successes - and learn from my many failures. I hate to see folks show up with little of nothing, because I know how humbling it is to ask for help on what should be simplistic and come as second nature.

Sadly, it seems belief we (sub)urbanites are really separated from Nature anymore, and we're fused to a modern routine. Even the act of making our own meals with basic ingredients and tools can seem almost improbable anymore, especially when a delivery guy or microwave can handle that for us with little skill. Fests are intended as spiritual, community-building vacations - not chores. If I can sway even one timid soul to leave their modern trappings behind and dance beneath the stars, then I've done my job. My hope is not to make any type of real profit off this book, but rather to simply share what I know with others, be they first-timers or well-seasoned veterans.

The first part of this book focuses on what to pack, ideas of where to go, what to do and what to expect. This includes my various vending, workshop, work shift, musical performance and facilitating experiences. The second part is about one of my many passions: Food! (I'm a native Chicagoan with the hard-voweled accent to prove it. Of course I like food!) I see so many people at fests "living" off energy bars and cans of ravioli, which is fine – but dull. While those things may provide basic sustenance, it's really no way to live, much less contribute to the community-building. Many wars have been settled over good food and drink, so I have made it a point to dedicate a large portion of this book to setting up a working outdoor kitchen (my altar) and what to create with it (my tools). I have never been much for following recipes, so writing them has been my greatest challenge and reward with writing this book.

Speaking of musical performances, you may be more familiar with me as a record producer. My husband and I run an independent record label- Rotting Corpse Records. Ron came up with the name from his love of zombie movies and heavy metal, and indeed the name *does* garner a bit more attention than the more subdued labels.

All of the bands on our label are comprised of exceptionally talented musicians within their genres, and their relationship to Divinity is of no consequence to us. Be they adherents of various denominations of Christianity, Paganism, Satanism, Agnosticism or even Atheism, what matters most to us is the members of the bands are good people at heart with a story to tell, brought to the forefront by their talents.

Of course, we do have certain caveats, as do all labels, one being we actually like their style of music - something that strikes a nerve and concerns (and perhaps even frightens!) the pearl-clutchers of society. (Oh my word!) Another non-negotiable detail is we absolutely have not, do not, or will not release anything we deem as hate-speech. What people want to do on their own time is perfectly legitimate; we don't have to like it. But, we will not fuel their insidiousness on our dime. Not only do we work with people who cross all sexual, racial and political lines, but if for any other reason, "it's just pain bad for business".

Deciding to write this book was actually a bit of an accident. On my personal site, I've been hand-coding my ramblings over the last seven years, just as things came to me. After a while, it became rather arduous to go back and forth into the site, so over the winter holidays, I decided to move everything over to blog format. I figured too, it would be nice to get some feedback via comment postings.

While I was moving things over, I searched the string "pagan camping", just to see if people even clicked over once in a while. Lo and behold, my camping section was the first and second result, with the third directing to it! The very first thing that came to mind was part of Sally Field's famous Oscar acceptance speech:

"*You like me! You really like me!*" I was completely blown away! I was certain actual festival listings would appear on the first page of results and probably even the second. I took that as a cue I should consider publishing my information, since people obviously find it useful. Then my Muse jumped on my shoulder and had me begin to frantically flesh out, edit and add more information until I felt I had covered just about every aspect I could. Whew! Who knew there was so much involved with this festival-going thing?

It's been quite the experience putting things together, and fortunately for me, running a record label has quite a few similarities to running a publishing company. In many cases, it's a different side of the same coin. Because of the existence and wide variety of Print on Demand companies out there today, thanks to our modern technology, I feel confident enough to go DIY on the matter. I've always been the independent type, and people who tell me I cannot or should not do something are my greatest sources of inspiration.

The way I see it, my information is not only for those who can afford it or whose libraries will carry it. Camping is for everyone who's physically able! In business terms, I see keeping the blog open as no different as when our bands post their music in streaming format - it's easy, free promotion. If someone likes something enough, they will buy it. And like I said, I'm not in this for the money. I'm not even looking at collecting adware pennies. I just really want to help people build community in relative comfort. So go ahead and pass this book around. No need to scan it; all the info is already online. My hope is maybe I will make a few more friends, and for me, that's the whole point of being a human being.

So hey, thank you for purchasing this book, and I hope to run into you at a fest in the very near future. If the tent's not a-shakin', stop on by my site!

A Guide to Pagan Camping

Part I

All About the Fest

> *"Reunion after long separation is even better than one's wedding night."*
> —Chinese Proverb

This first section of the book tackles just about every aspect of Pagan camping I could possibly think of. I'm sure I missed something here or there, perhaps even a whole topic I'd like to add in a future revision. So for that, *my bad*.

As with anything else I do in life, I like to compare what other people are saying about a topic. So if you doubt what I'm saying, want to call me out on something or just want further information, let the Internet, word of mouth and your own experiences be your guides.

I look forward to seeing you at a fest in the very near future!
–Lori

The Not-So-Inclusive Festival List

> *"Some national parks have long waiting lists for camping reservations. When you have to wait a year to sleep next to a tree, something is wrong."*
> –George Carlin

Here you will find a rather small, quasi-chronological listing of some of the more popular and/or longest running fests in the United States, most of which are of the primitive, outdoor camping variety. As you will see, I purposely omitted providing specific details other than their websites in anticipation of schedule changes and whatnot. It is absolutely imperative whatever fest you consider attending, you read their descriptions fully and contact the facilitators for any further questions, comments and concerns you may have.

And should you contact them with such questions, kindly do so in a polite and respectful manner, and be patient when waiting for a reply. These good and underappreciated people are the ones who provide the bases we need to make the magic happen, and a lot of what they do happens offline and away from cell phones.

- **PantheaCon** – www.PantheaCon.com
- **PhoenixPhyre** – www.PhoenixFestivals.com
- **Florida Pagan Gathering** – www.FlaPagan.org
- **Iowa Pagan Music Festival** – info.IowaPaganMusicFestival.org
- **Rites of Spring** – www.EarthSpirit.com/ros/rosb.html
- **Heartland Pagan Festival** – www.kchsa.org
- **Elf Fest** – www.ElvinHome.org
- **The Council of Magickal Arts** – www.magickal-arts.org
- **Moondance** – www.FaerieFaith.net/Moondance.html
- **Mountain Mysteries** – www.Mountain-Mysteries.com
- **FSG** (Free Spirit Gathering) – www.FreeSpiritGathering.org/fsg
- **PSG** (Pagan Spirit Gathering) – www.CircleSanctuary.org/psg
- **Music for the Earth** – www.OzarkAvalon.org/FestivalMenu.shtml
- **Starwood** – www.RosenComet.com/starwood
- **Summerstar Pagan Gathering** – www.SummerStar.org
- **Pan Pagan Festival** – www.MidwestPaganCouncil.org/festival.html
- **Sacred Harvest Festival** – www.HarmonyTribe.org
- **Dragon Fest** – www.DragonFest.org
- **Goddess Festival** – www.Goddess-Festival.com
- **Fall Fling** – www.FaerieFaith.net/FallFling.html
- **Pagan Fyre** – PaganFyre.ArkansasPagans.com

The Pagan Camping Checklist

"What [Lori] does is not camping!"

—Unknown

My Pagan camping checklist are on the following pages. Please feel free to adapt it to fit you/your group's needs. Some items may sound silly while others a no-brainer, but I based the list primarily off what I would ideally like to have on hand so as not to be a burden on and be able to assist others.

Also please note, items marked with an asterisk (*) are basic, major necessities, and items in bold are potentially large. Therefore, with a tent being basic and large, it is listed as such:

* **Tent** (large *and* important item)

- **Chair** (large but optional item)

* Duct tape (small but important item)

I would like to hope that doesn't confuse anyone.

Anyway, off you go to look at my list, hit a dollar, discount or thrift store to check things off. And, possibly you'll send me an indignant email about how I failed to list something you deem significant.

Sleeping
* Tent, Extra Stakes, Neon String/Lighting
* Sleeping Bag/Bedding
- Pillows
- Cot/Air Mattress
- Air Pump (batteries)
- Door Mat
- Whisk Broom and Dustpan
* Duct Tape
* Multi-Purpose Camp Tool (Hatchet, Shovel, Stake Puller, Mallet)

Hygiene
* Camp-Friendly Soap in Container, Wash Cloth/Scrubbie, Towel(s)
* Wet Wipes
* Camp-Friendly Shampoo/Conditioner, Hair Care Products
* Camp-Friendly Toothpaste, Toothbrush, Mouthwash, Dental Floss, Toothpicks
- Camp-Friendly Sanitary Products, Cotton Swabs and Baby Needs
* Prescriptions and OTC Medicines
- Camp-Friendly Shaving Supplies
- Shower Sandals (some types of daywear sandals can suffice)
- Nail Clipper, File
* Camp-Friendly Deodorant/Antiperspirant/Body Spray/Perfume
- Camp-Friendly Make-up, Brushes, Sharpener, Henna
* Camp-Friendly Insect Repellent
* Camp-Friendly Sun Block, Lotion, Aloe Vera/Sunburn Ointment, Lip Balm
* Camp-friendly Toilet Paper
* Clothes

> - Jeans/Sweatpants, (Hooded) Sweatshirts/Long-Sleeved Shirts
> - Shorts/Skirts/Kilts/Sarongs/Loin Cloths/Dresses, Coordinating Tops
> - Ritual Garments
> - Boots, Athletic Shoes and Sandals
> - Extra Socks (bagged separately) (wool and cotton)
> - Underwear, Sports Bras, Sunglasses
> - Umbrella/Poncho/Rain Coat, Galoshes/Wellies

* Laundry/Garbage/Wet Bags, Camp-Friendly Laundry Soap

Recreation/Road Trip
- Cards, Books, Magazines, Puzzles and Board Games
- Fishing/Hunting Gear
- Radio, CDs, MP3 Player
- Laptop/Game Player
- Camera

Other Essentials
- Lantern(s)/Flash Light(s)/Candles/Batteries
* 12' of Rope (clothes line, strapping, etc.)
* Folding Luggage Dolly
- Citronella Candles/Tiki Torches
* Cell Phone or Calling Card and Printed Map
* Picture ID and Camping Reservation
* First Aid Kit (aspirin, bandages, ointment, tweezers, scissors, etc.)
* Duffel/Sports Bag/Backpack (luggage)
- Purse/Tote/Fanny Pack/Mini Backpack

Comforts
- Cigarettes and Lighters, Ash Tray/Butt Container
* Pens and Notebook Paper
- **Ritual Items and Offerings** (travel altar, organic grass seed)
- **Drum, Acoustic Guitar**, Rattle, Whistle, etc.

Kitchen Needs
* **Food**

  - Perishable (fresh/frozen meats, dairy, eggs, some fruits, veggies and herbs)
  - (Near) Non-Perishable (canned, dried, citrus fruits, root veggies)
  - Drinks (hard/soft, hot/cold, mixes/brewables)
  - Snacks (crackers, trail mix, energy bars, dry cereal, fruit)
  - Seasonings, Oils and Condiments (mustard, ketchup, salt, pepper)

* **Large and/or Small Cooler with Ice**, Thermometer
* **Propane Range/Charcoal Grill/Hibachi**
* Canteen/Water Bottle

* **Picnic Basket or Chuck Box** (for toting miscellaneous kitchen needs)
- **Chair**
- **Card Table**
* **Camp Kitchen**
- **Cooking Needs**

   * Skillet, Sauce Pan/(camp) Dutch Oven, Tea Kettle and/or Coffee Pot
   - Potato Masher
   - Vegetable Peeler
   - Strainer/Colander
   - Measuring Cup/Spoons
   - Mixing/Serving Bowl(s)
   * Utility Kitchen Knife (santoku), Bread Knife
   - Barbecue Tools (tongs, grill brush, spatula, basting brush, fork)
   * Cutting Board(s)
   * Can and Bottle Opener
   - Zippered Plastic Bags (1 quart size are universal)
   * 2 Kitchen Cloths and/or Paper Towels
   - Skewers
   - Table Cloth and Table Clamps (vinyl for easy-clean purposes)
   * Charcoal/Lighter Fluid/**Propane**/Kindling, Lighters/Safety Matches
   * Aluminum Foil, Meat Thermometer

* 2 Wash Basins, Sponge/Rag, Camp-Friendly Dish Soap
* Place Setting/Mess Kit (plate, bowl, cup, utensils, napkin)

Checklist Details

"It is better to have something you don't need than to need something you don't have."
                                                            —English proverb

There are camping purists out there who will only bring what I denoted with an asterisk (*) on my checklist page and a combination pocket knife. These are folks who live off energy bars, dehydrated meals and plain ol' water from a running spring. And you know what, good for them. But for me (and I'm assuming, you, too, since you purchased this book) we or I want a few more creature comforts. I tend to lean on the Spartan side of things, but I like to think of myself as a *practical* minimalist. I needz to be comfortable, but I do so with dual- and triple-purpose items. There's that, and I'm not so much of a princess I feel the need to own twenty pairs of shoes, tons of clothes or crates of make-up, though I *do* enjoy being a girl all the same.

There's plenty more to put on the checklist, of course; just visit any camping store and see for yourself! But for primitive camping, I feel my list is more than satisfactory for the party-going Pagan. Also, please keep in mind many festivals do not let you drive in with a giant/obnoxious RV motor coach, as they simply do not have the space. However, many of them allow a van or *small* RV, if your reservation is made in advance, though hook-ups are rare. In other words, if you intend on traveling in such comfort and *style*, which I am not at all objecting to, be prepared to be "going dry".

Some items I have listed, like fishing and hunting gear, is obviously not intended for most festivals, unless you count these items as hunting for ummm... different types of game. (See my section on sex and sexuality for my opinions on that.) The list items are intended for coven retreats, field trips and family vacations, or however you see fit. Also, if you are camping in a group, not everyone is going to need to bring their own can opener; disregard that if your group is very territorial about their kitchen utensils.

I again cannot stress the importance of packing only what you really need to take with you. Yes, I listed a lot of stuff, but my list is intended to be cherry-picked based on your camping needs. The largest items really should be the first things you need to reserve for packing (again based upon your needs). Some items, like the generic term "food" I listed in bold, because I consider food to be one big item, rather than a bunch of individual ones. Therefore, items marked with * *and* is in bold are really what you need to try to pack first and work everything else around them. Of course, just like at the grocery store, the heaviest, sturdiest items go on the bottom, and the lightest, most fragile ones are nestled on top.

Another thing to bear in mind is how much space will be available to you at your campsite. If it's a family-style campground, go as far as your imagination can take you. However, if you'll be at a large festival, this just isn't going to happen. Even if you're the first arrival, you won't be well met with the others if you take up a football field for yourself. There will be others who (usually) will ask if they can set camp near you; go with it and make some new friends. If you're the lavish camper like I am, offer some of your community space, such as your kitchen set-up, to the light packers. Share a meal, loan a stake, help them set up; nothing strikes up conversation more than helping out.

Beyond the Big Three (food, shelter and clothing, which I'll discuss in a moment), everything else is pretty much a creature comfort. Basic knowledge of the outdoors, first aid treatment and good old fashioned common sense are what you need (like keeping hydrated and preventing sunburns). Take with you what you cannot do without, including everything you regularly use in your medicine cabinet. Pack all that up together in a bathroom kit, including first aid supplies, as well as bug spray and sunscreen. I wear powder foundation that provides sunscreen protection, so I count that as a double bonus for looking so damned fine.

A bathroom kit is a travel case of some sort that packs up just about everything one could possibly need in any location or circumstance. In mine, which I use year-round, I even included a mini blow dryer for cheap hotel stays, as a girl has to look her best. The one I use is a square make-up box that looks like a band's road case with accordion-style, fold-out compartments. How cool is *that*? If that isn't good enough for you macho men out there, you can also choose a tackle or tool box which serve the same purpose.

I mention this here, because it's a really good idea for every camper to have a bathroom kit of some form. Take a look in your bathroom and buy up travel size versions of the products you usually use. Just about anything you need can be found in travel/sample sizes, and yes, you can "steal" the soap and baby shampoo bottles from the hotels you stayed at. You *did* pay for them, after all. Also many department stores sell empty bottles of the see-through, trial size variety. Stock up on some of these and fill them up with your own products for only a buck a piece. This is especially good for those of you who make your own products, can only find your favorite brands in bulk containers or are strict adherents of animal-/earth-friendly products (which are not known for producing sample sizes). I did this last year to bring along my favorite bath scrub so I wouldn't have to settle on a second-rate product.

A camping shower kit you may want to invest in is specifically for the shower stalls. It's a wooden, slotted box, which looks like two (finished) pallets hinged together. The dimensions are roughly:

- 12" x 12" x 6" when closed
- 12" x 24" x 3" when open
- 3 - 3" x 12" x ½" planks serving as the slots on each "pallet"
- 3 - 3" x 12" x ½" planks secured beneath and across the planks for weight-bearing purposes (lattice fashion)
- 4 - 3" x 12" x ½" planks on each "pallet" for the frame.

The shower kit holds all of your basic toiletries inside, provided they are securely wrapped within your towel. And because the hinge opens up, it provides something to stand on (three inches off the ground) while in the stall. I've seen models sell for around $20, but I'm sure some nifty Pagan crafter can make one just as good - or better. (I've actually built one by sanding down two 25-CD crates, a couple of hinges and some extra wood on the backs to hold me up. It works great.

Here are its benefits:

- You make sure you grab everything with you the first time. (No "Shit! I forgot my soap box!" experiences as you're standing in the shower with dripping-wet hair.)
- Your feet won't have to touch that sometimes absolutely gross floor, even wearing shower shoes.
- For sanitary purposes, you won't have to worry about getting athlete's foot, especially if the water sloshes around.

Such a shower kit should be sanded well to avoid splinters, and heavier campers should consider using a stronger material with a non-skid surface. Slipping in the shower tends to ruin a fest.

Food, Clothing and Shelter

"Those who say 'You can't take it with you' never saw a car packed for a vacation trip."
—Unknown

This section is intended to cover the very, very basics of what I feel folks should bring to any Pagan festival that involves camping. I do get into some fun ideas and details as well, which is par to course with me. I never could be content with just getting by.

Your Tent and What to Do With It

Next to campfires, tents are probably the most iconic camping symbols out there. I believe it is the most important piece of camping gear you can own, and it is also probably your biggest item and investment. Yes, you can sleep under the stars with only a sleeping bag, or you can build a primitive shelter, but that's only if you also favor all of the other aspects of truly roughing it: Mosquitoes buzzing in your ear, ants tap dancing all over you, worms squirming on your fingers, ticks climbing in bed with you and burying their heads in your skin, raccoons tugging on your hair and spiders biting your face. Ewww - no thanks. All of these scenarios are pretty feasible to occur at a fest without a tent. Don't believe me? Just ask the guy who passed out in the field after drinking too much mead.

What makes a good tent? Well, a tent is supposed to serve the purpose of providing shelter, but there is so much more to it than that. When I look at a tent, I'm not only looking for something to keep the elements off me, but I'm also looking for some creature comforts. I like tents I can stand up in, especially when I get dressed in the morning. Sliding around on a slippery tarp floor, while pulling on a pair of jeans, is a pain in the ass.

While domes are perfectly fine, and yes, I own one as both a storage room and an overnight stay, I always go for the old-school models that require fighting with poles of various lengths. I also like the ones that have room dividers, preferably with separate entrances, so I can get dressed in an area where my covenmate, friend or family member doesn't have to see me squeeze into that too-tight pair of jeans. Those separate entrances have the extra bonus of allowing me to only disturb *half* my posse with a late night run to the privvies.

Since tents are so important, you have to be willing to invest in one that will serve your needs. I like nylon tents, because they're inexpensive, lightweight and compact, and they come in the most variety of sizes and styles. Dad was a canvas man. Canvas tents keep you much warmer at night, they're more rugged and durable, and if properly cared for, can last even decades. Think critically about these differences before investing in one, and spend some time online comparison shopping. If you are buying a new one, the best time to do it is right after Labor Day in the U.S. I purchased a large one for a mere pittance from its original price, less than even a little pup tent, and it wasn't even a return.

Now the *other* important thing I look for is how many people it's supposed to sleep. If the box says "Sleeps five to six", I count on that really being no more than three. Sure, you can cram that many people in there, especially if they're kids, but for the rest of us... not so much. I don't like walking all over people (and their bedding) just to get out, and I also try to avoid sleeping right on top of a tent wall. Moisture will collect on those walls from your warm body being up against it, which will make you wet and miserable. There's that, and you really have to keep in mind those walls are made of stitched canvas and/or nylon; water can *and will* get through those microscopic holes between threads if and when provoked.

The third thing I really look for is not so much name brand as the frills, since I'm not planning on sleeping in an Arctic zone in winter anytime soon. I want as many windows as possible, not only to have a view, but to get some friggin' air in there. The one I have now sleeps five to six, has that divider and also has windows everywhere, even up on top. On a warm summer's night, I can have all the windows unzipped, allowing in a cool breeze and a view of the stars. I live in a big city, so I never see stars (thanks to all of that light pollution). The tent came with a clear tarp that goes over the top in case of a sudden burst of rain. But when I'm fairly certain that won't happen, I don't bother clipping it on and have yet to get stung. (I'm sure Murphy and his Law will eventually catch up to my good fortune.)

One idea I now utilize (which I obtained from another Pagan camper) is to pitch a small dome tent so as not to hog up sleeping space with a bunch of crap. It also doubles as an additional shelter if a storm comes and the main tent gets all soggy. I say, if the camping space is available, use it, because those little dome tents do not take much packing space.

I've been eyeing all-in-one group tents for several years and truly want one, as they just seem to be the most practical for group camping purposes. I would want one that sleeps a minimum of five to six (which really means two to three), has a room divider and separate entrances, plus a screened-in front porch. Ideally, I'd want one that sleeps nine to ten with the attached storage space, just to have a place to tuck away dirty laundry and whatnot. Even when we camp, we like to be tidy, and smelly socks are best kept away from direct sleeping quarters.

The main reason I want such a sprawling estate is I think it would be really nice to have a "mud room" for shoes, as well as a place to play cards at night and to prepare an easy breakfast in the morning. I also really do like to create some indoor guest space that appears more like a studio apartment than an average tent. Of course, some people envision/utilize a yurt and its open floor plan, but I tend to appreciate a lot more privacy, which is a bit hard to come by without some sort of walls. Curtains can be hung on simple rods and would pack away rather easily; I could see that working out rather well, with a little extra work.

On a clear day before your journey, set up your tent to check everything is still in good repair, and hit the seams with some sealant. This is also a much better time to discover a tent pole is missing than when you arrive at the fest. It happened to us one year when I realized I had packed another person's long pole and he took my short one. If we had a pipe saw handy, we could have cut it down to size, but because it was only our shelter tent, we just made do by rigging up the one side.

If your tent is brand new out of the box, setting it up will also give you the time you need to slowly figure out how to do it in a cool and collected manner. The sealant will need several hours to dry anyway, so be sure you pick a spot that won't piss off the neighbors, even if it's at a park or nearby beach. We apartment dwellers need a place to set up, too, ya know.

Anytime you set up a tent, you need to be a bit critical of the area and the land directly beneath it. Isolated trees can serve as lightning rods, and even in good weather, camping under a bunch of trees can be dangerous, as heavy tree limbs can fall and crack you in the head. Being downhill always has the potential of water leaking under and inside your tent, and being downhill of the privvies is really a bad idea. Also, setting up your campsite near a deer path or other trails is usually not good. Besides the annoyance of people cutting through your site every five minutes (and they will be thinking you're a jerk for setting up there in the first place), deer antlers or claws (on raccoons and perhaps mountain lions) cutting through the nylon at night can really disturb your rest.

Flat, even surfaces, even just slightly elevated above the surrounding terrain, are ideal locations. Many people prefer choosing a spot over grass or straw, as it offers some padding on your tent floor. Be aware that padding can cause additional condensation, so an additional tarp beneath your tent can help prevent that. Be sure to remove any rocks, branches or anything sharp and pointy from where you will pitch your tent. You don't want to cut a hole through the floor and then perhaps even puncture your air mattress. Besides, holes are gateways for ants, ticks, spiders, mice and anything else that walks, crawls or slithers around out there.

Choose wisely where you want your door to be, including sunrises and direct daytime sun, and make sure there is a clear pathway to enter and exit. I prefer my door facing North – West as a second choice. Doormats are good indicators of this, and they offer a place to remove your shoes. If you are camping in a group, "circle the wagons" as they say, with every door facing toward the center where your firepit will be located. This will provide the greatest amount of open and walking space within the smallest footprint. (Yes, you can have your sprawling estate and keep your neighbors happy at the same time.) However, never build even a small fire within ten feet of anything flammable. Floating embers resting on sealant-treated canvas is bad. Really bad.

Pay careful attention to the prevailing winds as well, and use that direction to set up your kitchen instead, with the propane tank behind it. (This may be a bit tricky to keep the fire from blowing out, so you'll need to craft an aluminum foil fire ring around the flame.) This layout deters theft (yes, it occasionally happens), and it helps to build community, especially with your new neighbors camping near you. And, it helps to identify where you're at, especially if you decorate your site a bit. (See my section on dressing up your campsite for further details.)

Speaking of theft deterrence, don't bother with those little locks on the tent zippers. You may as well announce you have a dozen gold bars inside to anyone with a pocket knife handy.

While this may not be as big of an issue at Pagan fests as it is for other music festivals, not all magical folk are good or even neutral class. It is because of this risk vendors are usually permitted to park next to their sites, provided they make reservations in advance. *They* are more likely to have stuff they cannot afford to lose in comparison to the average camper. Theft risk is one of many reasons why I advocate personalizing your stuff, as well as shopping at thrift, discount and dollar stores for the bulk of your gear. There's no need to spend a fortune on things you'll only use once or twice a year.

When packing up your tent, don't worry if you can't get it to fit inside the box or duffel bag it came in. You may well discover folding it like a bed sheet will be easier to fit in your cargo space. When we were kids, Dad had us stomp out the air while he folded it up, mindful to keep the canvas side in and the tarp side out. This was only *after* he had checked everything was dried, zipped and swept up.

Stomping out the air was a lot of fun for us, though I do recall he wasn't entirely patient with our antics, treating the folded tent like a bounce house. He packed the folded tent in the trunk first, with the poles tied together (color coded with stickers), and the tent stakes, mallet and stake puller were wrapped in a little bag. Since we set up and tore down on a near daily basis, it was imperative we had such an efficient system. I still hear him in my head yelling at me about his system: "Don't put that there!" Okay, okay! (And then I'd go ahead and do it anyway.) Kids are indeed a joy and treasure.

If you have to pack up after an especially hard rain, or it's raining while you're packing, try to dry off some of the dampness with a bath towel during each fold. Canvas tents are especially prone to rot, mold and mildew, and it's the main reason why I don't like them. I can't stand that musty smell. When you get home, you will need to pitch your tent again until it has a chance to completely dry out. I know you're tired, and it's raining at home as well, but if you want your tent to last another trip or two, this step is non-negotiable. At the very least, pitch it in your living room (without the stakes of course) over an old blanket and run a box fan by it. If you have kids, they may even enjoy playing inside a while after it has finished drying. Have them help you fold it up like our dad did with us.

Bedding Basics

The next thing to chat about is bedding. What should you bring? Unless you don't mind the cold, hard ground, you're going to want to bring more than the sleeping bag you've had since you were a kid. Sleeping bags come in all shapes and sizes, as well as geared toward all types of weather. While I do own some sleeping bags, I tend to shun them now in favor of actual comforters and bed sheets. Why? Because I like air mattresses, and I like feeling more like I'm at home.

Speaking of which, I prefer air mattresses over other types of camp beds, like cots and rolls. Not only do they keep your body off the cool earth, which helps to prevent you from getting sick, but some varieties inflate to full-size beds. There are cots that do this, some with air mattresses on them, but because they take up so much space, many are impractical for packing in small vehicles.

Another thing I like about air mattresses is fitted bed sheets are no problem; yes, I prefer real bedding over sleeping bags. If you really dig sleeping bags, go for the rectangular kind that can be completely unzipped and zipped together to another one. That way, if you want to sleep with someone else, the two of you can comfortably snuggle together. Keep in mind, air mattresses can and will spring a leak, so keeping a patch kit on hand isn't such a bad idea.

Clothing: needs and wants

So now that you have your shelter tackled (and the comforts therein), you need to look at your second basic necessity: Clothing. Most people who have met me once or twice assume I only wear black concert shirts and jeans. Well yes, I do have over three hundred such shirts hanging in my closet, and I do spend more than I should on jeans, mostly because they actually accentuate my big, flat ass. But even this tomboy likes to girl it up some, and nowhere else is that more obvious than at places where I am bound to gather with a bunch of Pagans.

At festivals, I like to dress it up, especially for ritual or when vending. Mostly, I shoot for the practical. The following is going to lean on the practical so you can get a handle on how to pack wisely.

First off, most outdoor fests are held in high summer, out among the grasses and trees, and believe you me, it gets *hot* out there. While I'm not fond of white or pastel colors whatsoever, I will break my own fashion rule and go with the lightest-colored, most breathable clothes I can find. Sometimes, I'll wear very breathable black sun dresses just so I feel more like myself, or I'll opt for the halter top and sarong look. Men's cargo shorts are a favorite of mine, as they're nice and loose, and they sit on my mommy hips rather well, allowing me to make all those fabulous dishes with ease.

I also opt for sandals, especially my uber-cute gladiators, and not just because they're cute. Breathable sandals that have some type of *hold* on my feet are a lot less likely to slip off. And, because I have a medical issue, they surprisingly offer a lot more support and require less work than the beach-goers' favorites by keeping them on my feet while walking through the grass and muddy trails. I also prefer sandals in summer, as I can run my feet through the water to help cool my body down (even at the risk of looking silly).

Articles of clothing rarely discussed in terms of comfort are your undies, as many people tend to think fashion statement first. Cotton is best, as it doesn't cause chafing like those sexy lacy deals, and when cotton gets wet, it gets cold. So if you're really needing a bit of relief, peeling down to your bras and panties for a quick dip and then dressing again while wet will actually help drop your core temperature a notch. When I'm that hot, I don't care if I look like I entered a wet t-shirt contest. (Ladies, just stick with sports bras and leave the underwires for your nine to fives.)

Sunglasses, hats, head scarves and hair ties should all be on your packing list. Many of us, both men and women, have quite a bit of hair on our heads, and all that hair retains heat. On the hottest days, get your hair sopping wet and pull it back in a non-tangling hair tie; that too will help you handle the heat and humidity. My husband likes to wear baseball caps to prevent sunburn. He will also dunk his hat in a pool of water to help keep his head cool.

Besides shades and big floppy hats, you need to wear sun block, even if it's an overcast day. I wear powder makeup that not only keeps me looking so fine and prevents my skin from shining, but it also has a light sun block in it. I want a little vitamin D but not melanoma. I also use regular sun block on my arms, shoulders, legs (including the backs) and feet, anywhere my makeup wasn't used. I've gone without in the past and paid dearly for it the next day and through the week.

You're bound to discover lots of fun and shiny things to buy, and many workshops give you flyers and work sheets to take back with you. Needless to say, having something to carry all that stuff in makes perfect sense. Ron loves his multi-pocket backpack, while I prefer canvas bags and my now iconic handcuff handbag I made for myself. (I get at least one compliment a day.) Even if all you bring is a wallet, be sure it's secure. I've seen some rather creative ways to carry a pouch when nothing else was worn.

Also, make DEET your friend, or at least some other type of insect repellent. Besides mosquitoes, which will "wake up" as you pass through the low-lying flora they're resting in, remember there are also biting flies that feel like they're drilling right into you. If that's not enough encouragement, think about Lyme disease. It is my belief Ole Boy Murphy (whom some may also know as Loki) hand-delivers ticks at campsites right before we arrive - just to see what happens. (Ah yes, we're the butt of yet another cosmic joke. Yeah, thanks.) Be sure to have someone check you for ticks at the end of each day; you can make a flirty game of it if you wish, or you can visit the medic's office for a more professional evaluation.

If the fest is for a week, you can go with only packing three changes if you don't mind hand washing your clothes and drying them on a line. It will definitely save you some much-needed packing space, and it gives you a fun opportunity to dress up your site. However, light clothes aren't all you need to pack.

You'll also want to bring at least one thin, long-sleeved shirt for dusk when the mosquitoes come out. DEET is great stuff, though probably not the most earth-friendly, and even the most vigilant applicant will miss a spot. Just remember to bring some laundry detergent with you, because hand-/machine-washing your clothes take up less room in your trunk than piles of clothes... even if you use vacuum bags. (On that notion, remember to bring a line and some clothes pins, too.) Sarongs and wraps are always great for super hot days and take up very little room.

At night, switch over to your boots, jeans, hooded sweatshirts, socks and knit caps. These items you can probably get away with wearing twice without washing, provided you do not have a fear of deodorant. Even if it's the middle of August, you need to pack clothes for 30° F nights. By 3am, you just might be seeing your breath, so if you're not allergic or against animal products, consider wool. Wool has an opposite effect as cotton; when it gets wet, it actually warms up. Wool socks and boots are great for late night drum jams, but early evenings you can probably do just fine with the standard tube socks and sneakers.

So wait, did I just list *three* pairs of shoes? Yes, I did, and it was intentional. Ask anyone who has ever served in the military, and they will tell you the most important thing is to take care of your feet. When our son got back from Infantry training, his poor tootsies were incredibly beat up. It took over a month of me working on them before he finally began to get some feeling again from all the ruck marching. Yes, I suppose it could be said this progressive, modern woman literally served at a man's feet. Now granted, the most you'll probably be doing is spiral dancing your legs off and skipping merrily from one tent to another, but when your shoes get wet, you'll be glad you had another pair to wear. On that tangent, it is also advisable to pack each pair of socks in one of those plastic baggies, as there is bound to be rain at least once while you're at the fest. Outside of a good back scratch and uhhh... well, you know... nothing feels quite as good as getting out of cold, wet clothes and into some warm, dry ones.

Even if you intend to take the fest up on their option to not wear clothing, there is indeed a piece of cloth you still need to tote: A towel. No one wants to sit where your sweaty behind has been, and worse yet, no one wants to dine there. So please, do us all a favor and bring a plush towel with you, and don't let anyone dry themselves with it. If anything, it will feel a lot better on you than splinters.

Besides everything mentioned, a bit of rain gear, like a poncho, jacket or umbrella, and any ritual garb you wish to pack, you'll need one change of street clothes for the ride home. The clothes you drive home in should be fresh and clean, preferably bagged separately after washing. Why? While you may not notice it at the fest, you and everyone else is actually donning *Eau de Camp Fyre*, and the truck stop server will not find it arousing. Trust me on this.

The Food Department

At this point, all that's left to discuss regarding camping's Big Three is the food. This is one area I will be covering fairly well, so let's just chat about the gear *outside* the kitchen setup. You will need light to see what you're doing at night, but not so close as to bring the bugs into the pot. (Anyone who's ever attended a summer camp knows why they call the fruit-flavored soft drinks "bug juice".) You'll also need *something* to prepare your food on, and quite frankly, the ground just doesn't cut it for me. If where you're going doesn't provide a picnic table at your spot, and you're tight on cargo space (but not completely exhausted), even a folding card table will suffice.

Also, remember you do *not* need to bring *lots* of food. My husband prefers to handle the bulk of the shopping after setting camp - to get a break and cruise around the nearby town. I, on the other hand, like to be prepared and bring as much with me as possible. If space is an issue, you can leave the box of Sugar Frosted Corny Crisps behind and pick up one in town. Depending on the fest, you can hit the SuperMegaSaver before you enter the gates or after you set up camp – whichever is permissible and works best for you. Bags of groceries can always sit on passengers' laps right before arrival.

As far as what to cook with, that can be as simple or as elaborate as you can muster. If you plan on only cooking over an open fire, then you will need three things: Something to hold back the flames, a frying pan and a pot. A small shovel is good for digging out a pit, but if you don't have any rocks on hand, you're going to need to dig pretty deep and cover at least an inch with sand, gravel or dirt. And even with rocks surrounding your pit and a covered grill above the fire itself, you need to stay on top of that fire at all times with an extinguishing source at the ready. The reasons should be obvious but are often dismissed or forgotten: Roots in the ground can catch on fire, an ember can float onto your tent, and your flowy, drapy, Stevie Nicks-ish sleeves can have you headed for an emergency room.

The pots and pans you bring for the fire should be camping grade - cast iron if you can swing it. And yes, your utensils should be melt-proof and barbecue length, unless your stuff is made with commercial, non-stick coatings. If that's the case, keep that stuff away from your camp fire as much as possible; only use camp stoves. Whether you choose to go with propane (and propane accessories) or wood/charcoal, be sure to bring potholders and/or thick kitchen towels. You'll need something to grab a hold of everything.

I like cast iron skillets - a lot. Not only do they have that nostalgic look and appeal, but they sure do make the best tasting pancakes I've ever had. I also like the non-stick frying pan I have at home, because it's very light and is the only thing I can use to produce the picture-perfect omelet - food porn quality even. But when it comes to camping, for me, it really depends on my needs verses the space.

If I'm planning on just using my propane stove for cooking (or only using the fire for grilling/warmth/ritual), then I'm going to bring along my self-collapsible, aluminum non-stick camping cookware, especially if I'm only cooking for a couple people. This could be due to only going for a couple days, I'll be too busy vending to tend to a near-continuous fire, or I know it's going to be rather soggy. It didn't cost me much, it's still scratch-free, it packs very tightly in our little car, and it sure is easy to take care of. What's not to love?

For one thing, some people simply refuse to eat anything cooked on non-stick cookware, as that non-stick coating is very chemically-like. It's been said if you overheat something in a non-stick pan, the fumes released will kill your pet canary and extended use can even cause cancer. It's part of the same reason why some folks now shun microwave-popped popcorn. *What*?! Scary stuff indeed! Well, I still use my pan, and I still nuke popcorn, and I still smoke, so I guess *something* is going to kill me at sometime or another.

Another reason against non-stick cookware is more practical: It's easy to scratch, which then needs to be tossed, which then finds its way to landfills, which *then* needs to be replaced. The non-stick coating is very fragile, so you need to use special (plastic, rubber or wooden) utensils. One good scratch in the pan and into the trash it goes. Boo! Once that coating starts flaking or peeling off, and it doesn't take long for that to happen, the coating goes into your food. Yuk! I distinctly remember getting an order of scrambled eggs with "pepper" in it as a kid, but I found out later it wasn't pepper at all.

I almost hesitate to label this type of cookware as decidedly non-stick, because we've had non-stick cookware for over a century: Cast iron. A well-seasoned skillet is indeed non-stick, though like its modern counterpart, special care does need to be taken. Those things are heavy as Hell too, and everything gets very hot, including the handle, so they're a lot fussier in that department. But, they make excellent defense devices against home intruders, and regular use will reduce the arm reps at the gym. So yes, it has its benefits.

The main reason why I like cast iron is the same reason why I love my oven-safe glass stuff at home: It's versatile. Cast iron can be used on the stove top, oven and even over an open fire. Multi-purpose, baby. Yeah. And, both of them are tough as nails, so my clumsy butt won't easily break them. My non-stick stuff: Not so much.

The downside to cast iron again is maintenance. It will rust if you leave it on the rack to air dry, throw it in the dishwasher or otherwise fail to season it properly. Seasoning cast iron is easy; just grease it up with cooking oil and a paper towel and toss it in the oven at 200°F for a couple hours. (Be sure to place a cookie sheet below it to catch the oil drips.) In the time it takes to season a pan, you can catch up on your reading, watch a movie, read your bookmarked pages online or send a few well-constructed indignant emails or posts to the pet peeve persons or companies of your choice. After all: People are *always* being stoopid on Da Interwebz, right?

So really, this "battle of the cookware" is about weighing out the pros and cons and which is best for you as a result. As I said, I like both, and both have their issues. Now in regards to stainless steel... uhhh... I'll save that for another topic.

Since we're on the subject of *cooking*, let's talk about the stuff you use to *make* food with for a bit. Depending on which cooking surface you will be using, you'll need to use the appropriate utensils. Just like it's foolish to use a rock to pound in a tent stake for safety reasons (and a rock doesn't help you pull them out later), it's just as foolish to use the wrong cooking utensils. Ask any laborer, and they'll tell you: Always use the right tool for the right job.

As I mentioned previously, non-stick pans scratch easily, so it's imperative you choose your utensils carefully. Luckily, there is a rather versatile style of utensils out there that is both inexpensive and does not make Gaia cry: Wood. And, because I like to do things with *style*, I've found my wooden utensils are great for camp stove cooking, as they're just as lightweight and take up very little space. I still have my large plastic serving spoons, but I'm on the lookout for wooden variants to replace them, as the plastic ones are beginning to get pretty beat up. Besides, yelling at someone while shaking a wooden spoon at her is just so... so... retro.

For cooking anything over an open fire, wooden utensils are obviously your enemy. Fire likes wood - a lot. For this, I highly suggest using a set of barbecue utensils. I prefer to go with stainless steel here, because unlike cast iron, they can indeed hang out in hot soapy water for extended periods of time and air dry. I highly advocate barbecue sets because they're long and keep you and your drapy sleeves away from the flames. I bought a really sweet kit from a high-end outlet store several years ago for about five dollars, and they do their job with *style*. (There's that word again.) My set includes a two-pronged fork, a set of tongs, a spatula, a scrub brush and a basting brush; I'm on the lookout to add a stirring spoon that closely resembles the set, as I like to keep things looking good. *Must get thee off to the supply store.*

Besides the obvious just mentioned, you also want at least one good kitchen utility knife. Bringing only what you need is ideal, because each knife you bring has to be somehow guarded from damage and poking things, including you. My favorite one at home is called a santoku knife. It's quick to sharpen, it's light, it's not too big or small, and it chops, slices and dices anything its size with ease. With the exception of breads and large cuts of meat, I primarily use this single knife for just about everything. Because I value this one knife so much, I didn't cheap out on it and get a similar one advertised on TV. With knives, you really do get what you pay for. There are ceramic versions of these out there too, which need very little sharpening. If you have the extra cash and want to upgrade, visit a restaurant supply store.

You'll most likely also need a bread knife and a set of steak knives for your dining service. You can share these things, and I believe you can get away with cheaper serrated blade knives for camping purposes. Therefore, if you're looking to save some money, visit your local thrift store. I've found a complete service for four for only ten cents apiece, and usable serrated knives with decent handles can also be found at incredibly low prices.

If you have a good utility kitchen knife, you will need an equally good cutting board. *Please* don't cut on a plate or table. You will ruin your knives and everything you cut on it. I have a once beautiful wooden island here at home that now embarrasses me, thanks to the guys cutting on top of it over the years. It's not a butcher block, no matter how much they would like it to be.

For camping, the most portable and practical cutting boards are the plastic, bendable varieties. They're very thin, they're usually labeled for whichever food should be cut on it (to prevent cross-contamination), and because they're flexible, they make it easy to slide prepared food where it needs to go, rather than scooping. I wouldn't fold them for the trip however, as I wouldn't want to risk them retaining the folded shape.

Other cutting boards are available, with wood being the most popular and classic choice. I personally shy away from glass and granite, because they are bad for the knives, and because glass breaks. Then again, I'm not fond of bulky, heavy and/or easily breakable stuff for camping and traveling anyway.

And oh my yes - remember your can opener, collapsible strainer, serving utensils and dishes, as well as kitchen towels. I stress kitchen towels, because not only can you dry your hands with them, but they can keep your bread warm and even double as pot holders. For safety reasons, double the kitchen towels if you use them over or near an open fire. Burnt hands suck.

You'll notice on the checklist I mentioned a picnic basket. The classic styles available now are great for use all summer long. I picked one up at a designer outlet store for about $25, which came with service for four and is insulated to keep food fresh. I replaced the plastic-ware provided with actual silverware I pieced together at a thrift store.

Silverware is a lot thinner and therefore creates more packing space. There's that, and it looks nicer, and it's much easier to clean. I also ditched the cheap-looking dishes and swapped them for nicer, thinner ones as well, including the matching bowl addition. When camping, we use the picnic basket to pack the bulk of our kitchen utensils. The basket, keeps everything in one spot, and it gives my camp kitchen a bit of extra flair.

The following fits in my picnic basket:

- 4 plates
- 4 bowls
- 4 tumblers, 4 coffee mugs
- 20 pieces of silverware (tablespoons, teaspoons, forks butter knives, steak knives)
- Coffee pot
- Can opener

- Ladle, Spatula, 2 service spoons (one slotted for straining)
- Cutting board
- Dining napkins

Most of these items I purchased at thrift and dollar stores, so it wasn't all that expensive. The main reason why I like the picnic basket idea, which I got the idea from a former covenmate, is because it has snap latches to keep the dishes and glasses from shifting around. Even if they're not fine china, plates and glasses chip. I also pack cloth napkins, not only to be in *style*, but they take up the last bits of unused "dead" space and thereby also prevents damage from shifting.

An item Ron and I have acquired (and have fallen in love with) is a super-sturdy, fold-out, grated grill. We paid a mere $20 for it and is cast iron. It's really cool, because it takes up so little room in the car, it flips right over whatever fire you started on the ground, and, you can flip it on its side to keep shooting embers away while you let the flames lick your face. People have commented to us it resembles a cozy fireplace. What's actually funny is when we bring this out at music fests, where most attendees aren't big into camping, we always get this look like we invented fire or something.

I actually want to buy a few more to make a perfect enclosure for an instant campfire anywhere (where permissible), without having to scrounge for rocks and such. Then again, I might just go splurging again and buy a collapsible, portable, outdoor fireplace I've been eyeing at the discount store for about $100 and give the grill to a needy camper. (Can ya tell I'm a camping shopaholic?) I will add though, you need to have a bag of some sort to keep your grill in. Otherwise, soot will get all over your car. And no, I don't thoroughly clean my grill; I just give it a hard scrubbing with a grill brush. I follow the advice from that timeless sage, Al Bundy:

"*Last year's ashes make this year's burgers!*" Yes, they sure do.

And last but certainly not least, if you're *really* serious about camping for more than a couple days, I highly suggest investing in a camp kitchen. Before I got mine (as a Mother's Day gift some time back), cooking outdoors was a bit of a pain. My camp kitchen has a draining sink, an area to rest a propane grill and a separate prep area. It also holds all of my cooking utensils, it has a dish drying area, a paper towel holder/lantern/hot water shower clamp. There is even an added spice rack and a garbage bag holder - very convenient indeed.

Many of these kitchens set up in under ten minutes, and they collapse into themselves about the size of a small guitar case. Most currently run around seventy to eighty dollars, though more intricate designs are much more expensive. Therefore, t's definitely not an impulse buy. Just as you would with a group tent, be sure to research camp kitchens for features that will serve your needs best.

Miscellaneous Creature Comforts

Besides chairs, I usually bring my fold-out, scissor-style cot, since it has a dual purpose of serving as a couch and for putting my shoes on in the morning. However, I will leave it behind if space is a real issue. I also like lots of light, perhaps too much for some, and oh my yes, shade. (It's really not as contradictory as one may suspect.) If you like shade but don't have an outdoor tent (like a vendor's tent), even a tarp tied to some branches will work. Be sure to pack some rope for this and other needs.

If you plan on practicing ritual while you're camping, consider what's kosher and what's not. Is it cool to have a fire pit? Will your neighbors have a problem with heavy herbal smoke, such as from smudge sticks? Are you going to a family-style campground where you might get strange or dirty looks from other campers? If so, why not do something low-key? The Gods won't be offended if you don't have a big to-do over Them; They certainly will understand. A simple altar, decorated only with a plain cloth, a bit of food, a tiny lit candle and a single incense stick is just as impressive.

You may also be interested in bringing a travel altar, which is a mini altar setup that collapses back into itself. I have such a thing I use year-round at home which I created out of a milk crate, a statue, some mirrors, silk flowers and moss, with dollar store candle holders, tea lights and a pewter pentacle trinket box in the center. Everyone who's seen it says it's very beautiful and recognizably meaningful, though I must admit I don't believe it's quite road-worthy.

Were I to create another one just for the road, I'd perhaps use a water-proof shoebox, use aluminum foil pressed between clear yet firm plastic instead of mirrors, a picture backed on cardboard and laminated and unbreakable/fire-retardant candle holders/incense burners. (The trinket box is good to go however.) Whatever is meaningful to you, and whatever size altar you can fit are all that matters. Remember this: Just because it's simple or small does not mean it's insignificant.

Another item I own is a ceiling fan for the tent. It has a small LED light on it, so it's a nice two in one, and it attaches to the hook on top of more modern dome-style tents So many times I had complained about sleeping in a stuffy tent, and now I have a little relief, as it operates like an exhaust, sucking out some of the stifling heat up and out.. It does make a bit of a whizzing, humming noise from the fan, but for around $15, one can't expect perfection.

A remote–controlled lantern is a product I also now refuse to do without. They can be found rather inexpensively, and they sure do make late night dashes back from the privies much quicker and safer. By clicking the accompanying keychain in the general direction of my campsite, I stumble and struggle much less when returning, the same as I would click the keyless entry on a newer car at a crowded shopping mall. Sweet.

Side note: I came across this how-to link on constructing a primitive camping <u>air</u> <u>conditioner</u>! It reminds me of the ghetto a/c we put together as kids growing up. We would place a wet towel in front of a box fan and hope the breeze would cool us off a bit. (It only worked for about five minutes, but it was a saving grace!) It's supposed to drop the temp in your tent about 10°F. Even though that doesn't seem like much, going from 90°F to 80°F is a big deal, especially when there's a lot of humidity.

Thank you SnowCalla for such a brilliant idea! You can find the instructions at:

http://snowcalla.livejournal.com/605173.html

The Not-So-Hidden Costs of Pagan Festivals

"Stan, don't you know the first law of physics? Anything that's fun costs at least eight dollars!"
—Eric Cartman

Everyone knows an excursion of any kind costs money. Even a visit to the free zoo in town will still cost *something*, even if it's a day off work. So many tales of perpetual woe detail just how much a family trip can cost. Therefore, it should come as no surprise attending a Pagan fest is far from free. However, with proper planning and some bean counting, even a kid working part-time hustling coffee can make it to at least one fest a year.

The obvious place to start is where you want to go, and perhaps scale it down to where you can afford to go. If you have an older car, you may not want to drive it cross-country, unless you bring emergency funds. I have many memories of our dad driving us all over the United States in his 70's era luxury sedans in the 80's, sometimes towing a pop-up trailer. Those behemoths of the road usually made the trip with little more than a flat tire, but sometimes... yup, he had to dip into our vacation money.

If you're thinking of swapping a car with someone you trust, make sure both your insurance companies will agree to it. If not, renting a car is the next step, which can be rather costly. I'm pretty savvy when it comes to naming my own price on online hotel bidding, to where I have often landed hotel suites for a mere thirty dollars per night. It takes some work to play the game, as I usually have to visit daily with the same price until somebody caves in. I tend to start bidding a couple weeks out, as I know the companies get more and more desperate to book their rooms as the date approaches. I mention this, as the system works the same way for rental cars and flights, which I've fared decently there as well. So if you don't care what brand of vehicle you rent or the precise location, online bidding may be your best bet.

Now true, while many credit cards are supposed to cover your rental insurance, and certain degrees of personal auto insurance is supposed to be okay, notice how many times I've said *supposed to*. I'm a pretty smart and thrifty shopper and a shrewd business person to boot, but I've seen many car companies as being determined not to let you walk out the door without tacking on their insurance. That can cost thirteen dollars fifty cents per day. So, even if you nail a ten dollar per day rental package, add on that daily insurance cost, *plus* taxes and perhaps even mileage. Out of curiosity, I looked up my total costs for renting a work van for a week, considering I would want to drag both my gear and merch, and I was quoted between seven and nine hundred dollars. This doesn't count fuel, or food stops, or perhaps even a hotel stay due to arriving the night before the gates open. <u>Yikes</u>!

Therefore, if you don't think your vehicle will make it, and an extra grand isn't exactly lying around, see if you can get someone else to go with you. In exchange for their graciousness for them taking time off work and driving, you can offer to buy their ticket and share fuel costs and camping gear. If that seems to be *too* nice, just think of buying their ticket as covering for the wear and tear on their vehicle. Long trips weigh heavily on cars and on drivers alike.

If you cannot manage any of these suggestions, you may want to consider how far back you want to scale down your gear and hop on a bus. Many fests offer shuttle service, and buses are the least expensive mode of transit. There's that, and they usually has depots closest to remote festival locales. For me, it would work if I was *not* vending *and* joining up with a group that drove in so I could share their gear.

I once took a twelve hour round bus trip from Chicago to Knoxville, and while it wasn't the most pleasant experience in the world, it wasn't *that* bad in hindsight. The bus stopped periodically, which gave me time to get in a cigarette and stretch my legs - some stops long enough to get in a meal. I had snacks on me, as well as my cassette player (yeah, I'm "old") to keep me occupied. And while some guy took off his boots, making the bus smell like stale corn chips for the first hour, even the smell and the periodical crying baby didn't drive me all that crazy. I also took the red eye, so I slept for most of the ride.

So besides the admission ticket and traveling there and back, another major cost is going to be gear and food. I've covered both of these topics extensively, but I must stress the fact many fests do not offer re-admittance. The bigger fests have meal plans and little camp stores for items like tent stakes, tarps and duct tape, but that too can really drive up the costs, with the meal plans sometimes being up-front. (It helps the facilitators plan a bit more wisely, you see.) Because of this, I know people who begin saving and planning on the drive home for the following year.

As it is, I am beginning my planning now, just before the New Year, to see where I'll be able to, and afford to, go. I tuck away a bit of spending money, I reserve my vacation time way ahead of other employees, and I go through my gear and see where I can improve on it. Most companies do their yearly inventory checks this week/month for tax preparation purposes, as well as to investigate the biggest sellers and look to stock up on those items. So just like them, so should you take stock of your inventory. Camping gear is generally less expensive in winter, since most Americans don't want to buy a tent they won't use for several months. So if you can, try to get a bit of shopping done early.

If none of these options will work, perhaps a destination camping fest is simply not in the cards. That isn't a reason to not go; it's only limiting. Many fests and gatherings are held at hotels and convention centers, with complimentary shuttle service from the airport. Many too are located in your own communities at college campuses and community centers. And, some are held at private residences in a style reminiscent of slumber parties.

While I obviously advocate the camping aspect of fests and gatherings, it is my belief every person who identifies his/herself as Pagan in some way should leave the comfort of their homes, get off the grid and pitch a tent someplace.

In my case, my biggest hurdle is not *where* to go but *how* to get there. I'm pretty open to attending any event, though I have a few pilgrimages on my bucket list. I like checking out lots of different fests, even the weekend ones, because I meet lots of different people and learn new things. But, because we have a small, older car, I'm obviously limited on *space*. Who's going with me, how much do I have to take, and how long is it going to be. And, on top of my gear, I also have to somehow get my vending stuff packed.

Granted, I'm quite the digital Russian puzzle pro and a life-long apartment renter, so I consider myself an expert when it comes to making stuff fit. In fact, I consider it a challenge to rearrange the car several times over just to reclaim an inch of dead space. (I'm weird like that, I know). I'm also fond of dual- and triple-use items, though my hang-up is everything I do must be in, and with, *style*. (I'm far from the stereotypical dirty hippie, even when I try to be.) Therefore, whenever I come across a camping item that is both sturdy and replaces two, or even three, single items, or it can also be used year-round in the home, I'm on top of it - once the price comes down, of course.

The final not-so-hidden cost of Pagan festivals is the shopping. Oh my yes - shiny things! I must admit, after fifteen years, there isn't too much out there that charms me anymore or has any personal, intrinsic value. In fact, the last two years, I haven't found a single article, item or even trinket I really wanted at a Renaissance Faire, and last year, I really struggled to find just one thing I wanted at a fest. ("Meh I can easily make that. Meh, I have a better one. Meh. Meh. Meh.") Most books no longer interest me, because the bulk of them are Wicca 101-rehashed basics. I usually resell them online soon after reading them. As that pineapple-dwelling, chipper sea sponge says,

"I'm-ahhh... kinda picky."

At the bigger fests, I do tend to get drawn toward one thing or another, and unfortunately for me, they just so happen to be the most expensive things around. I don't believe in haggling over the price with a vendor, because I know what they go through to make them available to me. If *they* slash the prices on the last day, I just may take them up on their offer. Otherwise, I'll grab their business card and buy that special item at home down the road, perhaps with a nice customization. However, sometimes my thriftiness bites me in the ass, either in lack of availability or becoming a major project.

A few years ago, I was browsing around on an auction site, looking for a black leather corset that would suit me perfectly. As you may know, these things come in all shapes, sizes, colors, materials and price ranges. At a fest or Faire, a cheapie leather cincher can start at a hundred dollars. Well, I found exactly the one I've always wanted, and I know full well how much the corset I wanted runs - over four hundred dollars, sometimes up to a full grand.

The one I found online was a touch over a hundred, including shipping costs and just my size; what luck! Well, what should have been an easy process took threatening the seller with a charge-back before it finally arrived, well after the day I needed it. Boo! Several months later, I saw the online store went under, so that wasn't a shocker. Needless to say, you really do get what you pay for.

I hope the financial side of attending fests hasn't deterred you in any way. I know the economy sucks right now, with good friends of mine all but looking at overpasses as their new homes. Don't doubt for a minute the facilitators aren't hurting, or the vendors, or the performers. We're all in the same boat. But, Pagan festivals are more than just vacations; they're community builders and strengtheners - retreats we all need. Even if all you can genuinely afford is a one-day event in your home town, do it. I will say though it is again my belief getting even a few hours out and pitching a tent for a night will do your spirit much more good.

Packing Up and Heading Out

> "It's one hundred six miles to Chicago. We've got a full tank of gas, half a pack of cigarettes, it's dark, and we're wearing sunglasses."
>
> "Hit it."
> —Elwood and Jake Blues, *The Blues Brothers*

Let's say, for the sake of argument, you are coming from southern California and traveling by car to upstate New York. The festival is eight days long, and over a thousand people are expected to be in attendance. Will you drive straight through, trading off the driving and only stopping for gas and picnic meals? Or, are you going to make this a month-long deal, staying at five-star hotels, dining out for every meal, stopping at all the tiny tourist traps, antiquing and making merriment where ever you are? (Ahhh... I can dream, can't I?) Perhaps your road trip will be somewhere in-between? Also, do you plan on being the first one there to scope out the best spot, or are you into the whole Pagan Standard Time thing and just *love* to make an entrance? As you can see, there's lots of planning involved.

Even folks like my husband, who loves to be spontaneous, plans a little when it comes to road trips. You'll need to factor in how to pack everything, so that all your road gear is easily accessible, as well as keeping the heaviest gear on the bottom and lightest on top. You'll also need to make sure you have spending money and pocket change along the way. That chocolate bar at the rest stop is just screaming for you to buy it, but if you're only carrying $20's, you're probably not going to get it.

Once you have determined which items must go with you, try packing it in your car, keeping in mind how many seats will be holding people. Doesn't fit? Then something has to go; either your stuff or your car. Trailers and top cargo holders can help, but be sure your car can handle the weight. Remember to figure this out at least a week before you actually leave, because you don't want all your stuff sitting on the curb while you scratch your head.

Part of your road gear should also include beverages. Unless you plan on stopping to buy something every time you get thirsty, it's a good idea to pack a little cooler inside the car. I'm like a camel and rarely drink much, but even I do this. The big cooler can stay in the trunk, staying cold, and keeping the food from spoiling, and the little cooler is right by you, keeping you on the road and focused. Other items for your road trip should include a physical, printed map, cell phone, something to keep your passengers busy, and some of your bedding, like a pillow and throw blanket.

While packing, you may discover even the essentials catch you off-guard when determining space. If you are really strapped for space and feel it's a must, you can pack up your back seat to the ceiling, provided both your side mirrors are in clear view. Be aware changing lanes and backing up will take some adjustment, so only do this if state laws provide, *and* if you feel confident enough in your driving skills. If you make any stops along the way where you'll be out of the view of your car, make sure nothing valuable is in view, all the doors are locked, and the windows rolled up. Covering your gear with a bed sheet will camouflage your gear, as it will appear to look like bags of laundry and therefore not of much value. Don't be foolish and assume nothing will happen; respect Murphy's Law and you'll be just fine.

One very bulky yet light camping gear item everyone has trouble with is packing the sleeping bags. When we were kids, our parents would tuck these between the front and back seats in the car, since our little legs didn't need the room. We'd also unroll two more bags over the back seat and the tucked away bags, accounting for all four of them and thereby creating a twin bed for us to play and nap on. Of course, this was back before seat belt laws, but for children and smaller adults on long road trips, the comfort factor while buckled up still applies. Comfortable passengers equate to comfortable drives.

If, however, every ounce of space has already been dedicated, consider strapping your bedding onto the roof. Any truly watertight bag and strong strapping through cracked open windows will do, though you will need to note your maximum height. Some drive-through windows and sheltered parking lots are very low, so it is imperative you note this and do not forget. A sticky note with the height tacked to the dashboard is highly recommended. If you choose to go this route, also be sure to check your strappings at every stop.

Cleanliness is next to Godliness." How many times have you heard that before? When packing, it is vital to be as organized as humanly possible. Neatly folded clothes fit in your bag better, and soft bags verses hard-shell cases can accommodate more small items in odd spaces. Give your car an oil change, rotate the tires and get a tune-up. She needs it anyway. Wash your windshield often; car accidents can and do happen due to poor vision, with highway bug splatter tending to be the biggest culprit. While you're at it, take that squeegee to your turn signals and headlights. Those long, dark, winding roads will really need all the extra light they can get.

Also, by frequently cleaning out your car every time you gas up, you will feel better about the long drive ahead of you and knock out the lingering smells at the same time. Besides, who wants to open up the car door at a campsite and have fifty fast food containers come tumbling out behind you? With that in mind, give your car a good, hard car wash and vacuum before you arrive. Part of the festival is being seen; how nice it will be to have your first pictures taken looking good and feeling even better.

One final note: Please leave your animal companions behind with someone you trust. Many festivals do not permit them, and many campers do not like them. While you may think Anubis and Bast would like to romp and play in the outdoors, what they'll really appreciate is being quietly pampered by loving and caring sitters, in air conditioning, surrounded by their favorite toys and food.

Going as a Group

Many people who attend Pagan festivals do so in a group, be it their coven, their family or their friends/posse/entourage. Going in a group definitely has its benefits: You have someone else there to relieve the driving, you can all pool your resources and supplies, and you can work together with the setting up and tearing down. What you sacrifice in privacy you gain in spades with *help*. And, if you are meeting up with others at the fest, you get to (re)connect with people you may never otherwise get to see, and you get to share some communal space.

However, giving up some of that privacy can go south rather quickly, so it's a good idea to prepare yourself for the "what if's". Allow me to explain:

First off, who's going with you? If you're bringing your children, please Please PLEASE prepare them for what a Pagan festival entails. This isn't your standard family campground where societal norms exist. People may be running around in the buff, rather huggy-kissy, dressed rather strangely, and yes, rather inebriated. In a world where kids are raised to fear strangers, things can certainly appear to be turned on their heads. And, keep in mind too, kids like to blab about anything and everything. So when they go back to school and write their "What I Did on Summer Vacation" essays or fill in Gam-Gams, you might want to stress what goes on at a fest might not be a topic of conversation for everyone.

Also too, just as in "the real world", not everyone likes kids, and be as it may, there are some folks in our community who do not embrace the *Mother* aspect of the Triple Goddess within. Let's be honest: As a mom myself, who has been told numerous times our son was "an absolute angel" as a tyke compared to the more free-spirited types, even he got on some peoples' nerves. It sucks not everyone is as kid-friendly as we are, but that's just how it is.

Believe me - whenever I cringe and seethe at the store regarding an unruly child and *then* wonder how the parents can just ignore bad behavior, I get it. Kids spill their drinks - a lot. Kids are impulsive and need your undivided attention *NOW*. Kids get bored, occasionally at the most inconvenient times, and they aren't shy about letting you and everyone else know about it. And everyone's favorite, kids cry - loudly, sometimes complete with total meltdowns. Even for older children and teens, some of these same qualities can surface and then magnify in a world where everything they know has changed. Please think back to when you were a kid.

I know how hard it is to get someone to watch the kids for several days at a time. But, if you know in your heart your little angel is not going to be able to handle the plethora of societal changes that encompasses a Pagan fest, it might be a better idea to make such arrangements. Being in a safe, familiar and comfortable environment with routine might be what they really need. Or, take them to a family-themed campground when you return so they aren't deprived of an outdoor excursion. It is my opinion every child should spend some time in a tent, even if it's only once and only for a night or two. Of course, this again also goes for your fur-babies. That is, if they're permitted to attend in the first place. Be sure to check.

If you think I'm picking on the 'rents, I'm really not. As a mom of a now adult son, who was raised in an openly practicing Pagan family deeply rooted in the everyday, please believe me when I say I'm speaking from past experiences and from the heart. I'm genuinely being practical, honest and fair. To further back that up, let's critically explore what it would be like for our friends, relatives and covenmates. If they've never been to a Pagan fest, make sure they've reviewed the details ahead of time and have gotten some feedback from various sources. (Ain't Internet searches grand?)

If your potential adult guests are humming and hawing about going, don't plead, hype up, force, guilt trip or otherwise push them into going. Not only is it bad manners, but they just may be trying to let you down easy it's not their thing. Pagan festivals are not for everyone, even for people who otherwise enjoy camping. While I think they're incredibly awesome, some people don't like it, or an important aspect of it, whatsoever. Look at it this way: Don't *you* hate being dragged someplace? Why do it to someone else? It's called respect, not to mention tolerance and understanding. On that notion, if your coven makes attending fests a requirement, make sure that rule is made distinctly aware from the get-go, and don't change the rules along the way without unanimous agreement.

To counteract all that negativity, if everyone in your group is indeed psyched up and rearing to go, plan, plan and plan some more. You want to get the most out of the event, and so does your group. I've already discussed this stuff in detail, but I want to reiterate how important preparation really is. Going anywhere on hyped up expectations and sheer bliss can go south really fast. Bring some comforts of home with you and personal activity supplies, even if you get a sneer like I occasionally do.

- If the kids want their music and video players, let them bring them. This of course is provided you have a way to hook up to the electricity needed or have enough batteries. Otherwise, have *them* figure out what *they* want to do for their own entertainment.

- If your covenmate wants to dress in street clothes for the duration, don't look down your nose at her. It's her body, not yours.

- If your brother insists upon some fast food along the way, hitting a drive-thru off the Interstate isn't going to knock too much time off the schedule.

- If your husband will not go without his death metal jams, is it really doing to annihilate your vibe to let him pick every other CD? The switch between Pagan folk music and brutal death metal will, at the very least, make the long drive *interesting* and perhaps will even help pass the time through corn country.

Compromise is the key to diversity, and it's the building block of tolerance, which tends to lead to acceptance.

Speaking of compromises, this includes what to do while you're at the fest. If you're the only one who wants to attend the tantra workshop, don't force your husband to go along. Just have him snooze out for a while and fill him in on the new techniques you learned later. Likewise, if you're not into the goth/folk set that night, offer to get dinner going while your covenmate ebbs and flows in the crowd. And too, just because your brother wants to be on recycling patrol, that doesn't mean you have to sign up for the same work shift. Hint to him he just might meet that special someone while sorting the green bottles from the brown ones.

To sum things up:

Discuss - Plan – Compromise.

Festival Dos and Don'ts

> *"Nag, nag, nag."*
> –Ben Shockley, *The Gauntlet*

I suppose this is as good a time as any to lay out some ground rules, and general proper etiquette. As you know, there are different rules for traditional vacation camping than festival-going, so I'm going to include both. Most of this is common sense, but unfortunately, there's always that one guy who needs to be reminded on more than one occasion.

These are in no particular order - just as the thought crossed my mind.

- Are you a smoker like me? Then be considerate, both to the non's as well as to Nature Herself. Don't blow smoke in someone's face, don't smoke in areas you're asked not to, and don't flick your butt just any ol' place. This reminds me of Eddie Murphy's character Billie Ray Valentine yelling at his party guests in the movie *Trading Places*:

"What is this? What IS this? Wait, man! Wait! Hold up! Who be puttin' their coals out on my floor?!" Do you think Nature thinks any differently? A good and easy way to remedy this is to pack a plastic soda bottle in your fanny pack or purse, with a little water in it. When you're done with your cigarette, simply toss it in your bottle and give it a swirl. Discard the "butt juice" the next time you get into town. No fuss, no muss. For you non-smokers, please don't nag us about our health. We know it's bad for us;

we don't need our mom following us around when we're trying to have fun. If it bothers you, and we're in a smoking area, then don't stand next to us. Simple enough, right?

On the cleanliness tangent again, I must remind everyone not to be a Piggy Pagan. Leave the Earth better than you found it. Toss a little grass seed where you camped (if that's permissible). Use the recycling bins <u>correctly</u>; if you don't know, ask. And while it may be tempting, don't carve or write your name on anything living and anywhere where it isn't permitted; that's called graffiti.

- A big reason why many folks turn to Paganism, in all its guises, is for religious freedom. Respecting the beliefs of others is a big deal at festivals. If you're a Faerie Wiccan, don't expect a lodge member of the O.T.O. to want to call on woodland creatures as Deities. And, if you're that Thelemite, don't roll your eyes at the "fluffy bunny". We all have our beliefs, and they're all just as valid. I lean on the darker things in life, but every now and again, I too like a bright, sunny day.

- Sexual freedom is another thing many Pagans enjoy, but with freedom of any kind comes responsibility. I am happily married and completely monogamous, whether hubby's with me or not. Therefore, I do not appreciate advances made at me when these facts are known. However, what you wish to do with a willing partner (or two) is totally fine by me.

- A side note on that is in regards to the "clothing optional" festivals. I'm a surprisingly shy person when it comes to my own skin, but that doesn't mean I have a problem with what other people want to do. For those of you who aren't used to seeing mams displayed outside of those late night TV ads, this can at first be a little jarring, but even I get used to it after a half an hour.

Please act in an adult manner, even if you really have to hold back a giggle or goofy grin. After all, in nature, you are the odd man out for feeling the need to cover up what you were born

A Guide to Pagan Camping

with. If you bring your kids, they need to be aware of this fact ahead of time. If you don't think it's appropriate for them, or if they say it would make them feel uncomfortable, then don't bring them. Respect goes a long way, no matter whom or how old you are.

- Ask before you take someone's picture (or publish one); not everyone is open about their faith. Some people are not "out of the broom closet", which could cause them some backlash. There's that, and well, it's just plain rude.

- Yes, there be shiny things a-plenty, but never assume it's okay to pick them up and handle them. You can make a comment on something, but never assume it is okay to grab it, even if the item in question is on a merch table. You see, if you arbitrarily scoop up someone's wand, you just put your energy into it, and that's just not cool.

- If you feel like taking the folks up on the clothing option, please be aware of where you're walking around. Some areas are for clothed folks only. And even in the free zones, it's kind of gross to plop your bare ass on a chair or table. I'm not fond of the scent of ball soup before meals. Bring a towel.

- If you walk by folks "zoning out", leave them be, unless they appear to be in need of medical assistance. Maybe they're meditating. Maybe they're sunbathing. Maybe they're just catching up on some Zzzz's. Whatever the case may be, consider that your Do Not Disturb sign. But again, if the person you come across appears to be passed out in the middle of the road, use your common sense and help him.

- To eat meat, or not to eat meat; that is the burning question at many a festival. Me personally, I'm a vegetarian, but I can make do with just about anything presented to me; I'll pick it out, or I'll stick with the sides. The way I see it is this: If someone went through the trouble to make me a meal, and it's obviously out of love or friendship, then bless the soul who thought that much of me. I'll simply eat around the sausage and thank them for their hospitality.

I also do not drink anything *soft* with sugar in it (alcohol not included). However, if someone offered me a drink, and she only had a cola (and I'm really thirsty), I'll drink the cola.

I do not believe because one group of people has dietary restrictions, either for health or conscious reasons, I need to cater to them. Therefore, when I offer my potlucks, I offer it because I like it and I think someone else will, too. I do provide a list of ingredients, just to shave off a few (repeated) questions, usually in recipe format. Besides, if there is absolutely nothing else offered there I find appetizing, at least I know I can eat what I brought and not go hungry.

- The common rule at drumming circles is the dancers always have the right of way. Drumming and dancing around huge bonfires with hundreds of people, some infused with alcohol, some even juggling the flames themselves, are big parts of the evenings at Pagan festivals. People become frenzied and sometimes forget where they are. The dancers quite frequently go into a semi- or full-trance state, so it's imperative to let them have plenty of room. If you need to get to the other side of the bonfire, please walk around.

- People who get into drumming are encouraged to pack their instruments and bring them with to the drumming areas. When you get the feel for the rhythm of the beat, join in. Sometimes the pace is slow, sometimes it's fast, and the beat frequently changes tempo throughout. If you fall out of time with the other drummers, brush it off, give yourself a quick breather and join in again. It's really no big deal. Even A-List professional musicians have that happen on occasion. (Trust me: I should know.)

- Drumming, or course, does not mean you need to limit yourself to just drums. People who are good with wind instruments, such as flutes, penny whistles and recorders, are also encouraged. Be there with bells on and dance while you add to the beat.

A Guide to Pagan Camping 55

Rattles and other types of shaking instruments are perfect for adding a subtle, yet powerful, background sound to heighten everyone's most primal emotions. The many layers of sound drawn from drumming circles can be both heard and felt from miles around, so be a part of it.

- Try to remember though, not everyone can keep up with the night owls and will find themselves retiring to their woodland abodes. While I personally find background drumming and a soft orange glow to be the most incredible way to be lulled to sleep, some need nearly complete quiet and darkness. Therefore, please keep the drumming to the drumming circle after midnight (or whenever posted) for the light sleepers.

In retrospect, the light sleepers should have their camp site as far away from the designated drumming circle as possible. Packing ear plugs and/or night masks is highly advisable, because if the night owls don't wake ya, the birds and morning sun will.

- Loud noises at night also include people who can get rather loud and boisterous when having a good time, especially while drinking. Those who invoke animal spirits need to also be conscious of this. While I personally think it's neat to hear wolf cries back and forth between physical and astral beasts, some find it rather disheartening and would rather hear nothing but their own snoring. This also includes using any unauthorized amplified sound, including the monstrous car sub woofers down to a little boom box. Radios are encouraged for checking in on the weather and such, and okay at most regular camp grounds, but are not permitted at many Pagan festivals.

- Mornings around any campground are also usually semi-quiet, as most campers I know are up at all hours and sleep in. Why not? They're on vacation, right? Me, I'm up the minute the sun shines in my tent (or when it starts heating up). Early-bird me keeps that in mind, and keeps the hollerin' to a lull. In other words, please don't shout "DO YOU WANT YOUR EGGS UP

OR OVER EASY?" to your covenmate who's fetching water across the field. Ask him before he leaves.

- Okay, one more bit about noise, and I'm outta here. This is directed at you frisky folks. I'm so very happy you two were able to reach an incredible, simultaneous climax - they're rare and should be cherished. Good for you. Also, I'm sorry *you* over there felt your lover doesn't meet up with your expectations anymore - it sucks, I'm sure. Either way, most folks don't want to hear the moaning and bitching.

One fest we attended, the woman in the next tent over was repeatedly yelling,

"C'MON! F*** ME, DAMNIT!" and her beau was replying,

"I DON'T FEEL LIKE IT NOW!" This went on and on throughout the night. Ron and I, while we first got quite the laugh regarding this "conversation", we later agreed it was both inappropriate and nauseating by the end of the fest.

So please, no panting after 2am and keep your private issues... private.

- When drinking out of the communal chalice, it's a good idea to wipe it before and after you drink. (There's that, and it makes you look like a good circle mate as well.) If you have a cold, please don't drink out of it. One ritual I was at, it was suggested folks could raise the chalice to their foreheads and put forth their energy in that way.

- Finally, and this is really out of common sense: Remember where your camp site is and what your tent looks like. Night time in the woods gets *really* dark, so I like to tag my tent ropes with neon tape or string to find my site (and the ropes as well). In the day, it adds a little flair to my site as well. If the site is well-lit or your tent is fairly isolated, then this isn't as much of an issue.

Arriving at the Fest!

> *"If we really think that home is elsewhere and that this life is a 'wandering to find home,' why should we not look forward to the arrival?"*
>
> —C. S. Lewis

Okay, so one last glance at the map, one quick bathroom break at a gas station, one more turn of the road, and finally you're there. Are you early? Make the most of it. If you brought your camping stove or mini grill (if the grounds allow you to use that and have a place for the hot coals), you can whip out that bad boy and start a tailgate party. Pull out a couple chairs, lounge back, drum a little, whatever you like. Keep an eye on the clock though, because about a half hour before the gates open, you'll want to pack back up to drive in and unload. You don't want to be holding up everyone else.

While you're waiting, dig out your photo ID and your camping reservation. A sign-up sheet may also be visible for work duty. If you are early enough to snag a fun job, the work period can be a great way to meet others. It's usually no more than a couple hours all together, and it's really helpful in keeping the self-sufficient festival running. (*Pssst! The tear-down job might offer you an extra night.*)

Remember most festivals aren't going to allow you to have your car parked right beside you. Some let you drive in to unload, others make you drag everything in bit by bit. If you know the situation ahead of time, you can be prepared by having something to make the trek a little easier. Those nifty luggage dollies you see the airline and legal folks pulling behind them are great;

they fold up small and are surprisingly strong. My large cooler has sand-capable wheels on it with a collapsing handle; I would need a second set of hands otherwise. This thing is so cool that you can actually double it as a dolly. Just load up some stuff on top of the cooler, and then strap some bungee cords over your load. Hey - when you're trying to make as few trips as possible, you're going to take <u>everything</u> into consideration.

One of the reasons for being early or on-time is to scope out the best spot. That's the first thing you're going to want to consider. Are you a sun-worshipper or a tree hugger? Sunny spots are more central and away from bugs (but hot); shady spots are more secluded and more in tune with Nature. The other thing is for you festival-going merchants; they usually have their own designated area.

The other reason is kind of a given: You want as many daylight hours to calmly set up camp. I can't remember how many times I've had to set up in the dark. The cartoonish grumbling my dad used to parody rings in my ears just thinking about it. Are you going to designate the major jobs, or is everyone chipping in equally? I've found that it works well either way, depending on the group. Once you are set up, you're going to want to step back and admire your site. (And remember, your site would be even *more* admirable and picture-worthy if you string up a banner or something to designate your Coven or group.) Relax a while, pop back a cold one and wave at other campers as they start to meander throughout the grounds.

Depending on the festivities planned, and at what time you're all settled in, you may want to start getting lunch or dinner together - your first grand feast on a job well done. Food is such an inherent part of community; wars have been settled over a good meal and drink. Please refer to my Part II section for ideas on alternatives to hot dogs and beans.

So now that you're all settled, you have a full belly and you're finally starting to reap the rewards for all that driving and planning... now what? Well, if you're at a festival, there'll either be postings or a herald letting you know of the different activities you can participate in. Grab a pad and pencil and jot down what you'd like to do, its location and at what time it's happening. Otherwise, gather up your group and go for a quick hike through the little village that is popping up around you and meet your new neighbors. If you're on a conventional vacation, stop by the visitor's center and grab up some brochures. There are plenty of valuable coupons you'll want to snag there as well.

Where to Set Up Camp

Where you camp should be just as much a part of your prep as choosing which work shift to take. After all, the spot you pick is going to become your home, be it for a weekend or a week. Time will fly while you are on it, but the ground that welcomes you will remain in your heart for a lifetime.

The way I figure out where I want to be, if I've never been there before, is by narrowing down my choices by process of elimination, provided I have every option open. I do this with a map of the grounds. Here's what I look for as an example:

- **Open or Pre-Designated**: pre-designated
-- **Sun or Shade**: shade
--- **Main Strip or Hidden**: main strip
---- **Hook-ups or Primitive**: hook-ups
----- **Near Restrooms/Showers/Water Access?**: no

The bigger fests have pre-designated areas, such as for the vendors, recovering alcoholics, the LGBT community, kid-/family-friendly, handicapped accessible and whether or not one likes being near the drumming area. These types of spots need to be requested when you submit your application so the facilitators can save it for you, though it's still a good idea to show up as early as possible. Also, if you're going in a group, or if (part of) your group is meeting you there, you may be able to request space for X amount of tents and create your own spot. Generally, spots not designated by the facilitators are on a first come, first served basis, but returning encampments over several years are typically respected as pre-designated.

For myself, I like being in the shade whenever possible so my tent doesn't heat up as badly. If I'm vending, I'm obviously going to be placed in the vending area, and I want to be right in the middle of the most action, preferably by the stage. But even within the vending area, I still generally get my pick of sun or shade, so as long as I show up early enough. (I've always been a bit of a Time Nazi, even as a little kid, so I tend to arrive for everything early.) I'm physically capable, and I don't like being anywhere near pools of water, so I leave those spots alone. Also, since I want one of the few vending spots that provides electricity, and I still want some shade, my spot has now been whittled down to spot #74 or 75.

Now even if I were to be guaranteed spot #74, I still intend to show up early, even if I wasn't such a Time Nazi. The reason is because I like having as much time as possible to get everything just so. I want to make sure there aren't any rocks under where my tent will be, and I also want to have it on as level ground as possible. So many people overlook these things when setting up, even people who've gone camping several times. But before I pitch my tent, I have to set up my merch section, as close to the road as possible, and I work around my camping space from there. Plus too, if I'm allowed to build a fire, I need to make sure where I build it is not under any low lying branches.

Having the choice between #74 and 75, I also will want to get there early to see who is setting up at #73 and 76. Not only would I want to scope out my choices, but as a vendor, I want to get an idea of who would be my immediate neighbor. I mainly sell CDs, so I want to put a gap between my booth and someone else who also has them. I don't want to confuse the customers. I also would prefer working next to someone who I already know or have *some* stuff in common with them.

Trust me, it really sucks to be perched on a stool all day next to someone who is a polar opposite, or worse, someone who will bitch/nag/whine/guilt trip about one of my habits or personality. Boo! I've been there, I've done that, and I'd rather not return. The way I see it, I may be working, but I'm also on vacation. I get that type of behavior the rest of the year, so why deal with it now when I'm supposed to be enjoying myself? That's rather... *illogical*, as a pointy-eared Nemoy would say.

As you can see, there are plenty of things to consider when choosing your camping spot, even if you're not going to any type of a pre-designated area. Going, or meeting up, with a group will provide a buffer from people who don't particularly mesh with your habits and personality, and at the same time, you'll create a community *within* the Pagan community at large. Think of it as living in a condo building within a desirable neighborhood. Before you arrive, you can *and should* ask questions about a location you think you would like, as that's part of what the facilitators are for: To help you enjoy your stay make your time at the fest memorable.

Camp Kitchen Preparation

"Although I don't take myself very seriously, I do take my work extraordinarily seriously."
–Alton Brown

A week before you leave home, I highly suggest to plan a menu, especially if you are going with others. (See my Sample Menu for plenty of tips!) Nothing is worse than having to run out to the store at the last second because you either forgot one lousy item, or worse, you didn't bring enough food for everyone. It's also a good idea, especially with others, so you can discuss likes, dislikes and allergies.

What I did in the past was I wrote down what I would like to have, and then allowed everyone to decide if that was satisfactory with them. If that doesn't work for your group, ask them for any suggestions to alternate the basic menu. (Hey, if you have the kitchen duties, you might as well enjoy what you're doing.) Remember if you have a large enough variety, you should be safe with most items. Also, by doing it this way, you've cut out a large chunk of everything there is in the world to make. It may be more diplomatic to have everyone write down meals on a slip of paper and drop it in a hat, but someone has to make it.

Once the menu is settled, write down a comprehensive shopping list and <u>stick to it</u>. You'll want to show your group how much you paid so you can get partially reimbursed. Be sure to hunt for sale and generic items as much as possible gourmet doesn't have to mean pricey. Go alone, if possible. The more people you bring with you to the store, the more likely you are to "give in" and steer away from the shopping list.

The night before you head out, have everyone meet at one location with all of their gear. Have a kitchen party by having everyone pitch in with the prep work and adding their magic to the food. Don't forget to make a good meal for yourselves beforehand; the less hungry you are, the less likely you are to "graze" in the kitchen. Also remember to bag everything up, either to be refrigerated or frozen. Squeeze out as much air as possible; this prevents spoilage as well as reduces the amount of space you'll need in the cooler. Remember not to over-pack, either with your gear or your food; that, and all of you, need to fit in the car, too. There's nothing wrong with picking up a few items in town after setting camp, especially perishables and bulky items, such as boxes of pasta and paper towels.

And yes, definitely: Remember to double-check you have everything for your kitchen set-up before you drive off. Even if it's just you, and a couple of your meals are merely cans of ravioli, you're going to need your can opener to eat it. Be sure you have stuff to cut with and on and that it's SAFELY tucked away, stuff to cook with and on, stuff to eat with and on, and stuff to prepare and clean up with. Just as you have used your zipped freezer bags to conserve space, so should you do that with the rest of your kitchen ware.

One idea I have, besides owning a camp kitchen, is to pack some items in milk crates. They're strong, weighted down and small enough to reorganize while packing the car. At the fest, they will double as a stackable pantry, especially for quickly hauling in goods for those freak storms that come in out of nowhere. I've discovered one milk crate holds twenty four standard-sized cans, plus twelve half-sized cans, such as tomato sauce or mushrooms. Other crates can be used to store pancake mix, dried beans and loose kitchen utensils. The best part is, by having several crates side by side, they create a whole extra level on top for tall stuff like cereal boxes.

One more thing: Don't be a Piggy Pagan - clean up after yourself. Reduce, reuse and recycle. Bring only what you really need, and only what you can wash, rather than throw away.

Many festival sites ask you to bring your garbage home with you, so make sure you have as little as possible. Save up a few plastic grocery bags; bring them with as garbage bags, as well as for your dirty and wet laundry. Also, most campsites and festival grounds offer recycling bins - use them.

Keeping Food Safe

Most people should be aware how important it is to store and prepare food properly, and nowhere is that more vitally important than anytime we're away from home. The way I figure it, if I catch the stomach flu from a local restaurant, at least I have the consolation of dealing with such an unpleasant (and sometimes downright violent) sickness in my own home. Just the thought of being outdoors with the bug makes me want to scrub my veggies extra hard.

Just remember these basic rules:

- Hot food stays hot, cold food stays cold.
- When in doubt, throw it out.
- Keep it clean, keep it green.

Canned and non-perishable foods tend to be camping staples, but even these need some attention. Any canned food that bulges, leaks, foams or otherwise smells funny when opened should be immediately discarded. Many containers have various "Sell By" dates, which do not necessarily mean they are expired beyond those dates. However, I tend to abide by them rather than take any risks. Brown rice, and anything with natural oils in them, will go rancid if improperly stored or stored too long.

Raw, fresh fruits and vegetables can be stored without refrigeration until they're ready to be washed and eaten. Some foods tend to ripen and/or rot much quicker than others, and heat tends to escalate things. If you would like to bring bananas, buy them bright green and suspend them at your site if possible.

(Durable clothes lines can act as banana trees.) This will help ensure they do not ripen or bruise before you even get a chance to eat them.

Citrus fruits, with their hardy skins, tend to handle the heat and traveling best, while leafy greens and thin-skinned fruits and veggies sometimes appear to go south as soon as they're plucked from the garden. Wrapping celery in aluminum foil and packed at the top of the cooler will keep it crisp longer, and lettuce will survive longer if wrapped in a paper bag, rotated daily and also stored on top. Root veggies prefer cool, dark and dryer areas, like the environments in which they grew. Storing them in a ventilated cardboard box in the shade will help keep your potatoes from spudding.

Fresh meats need to be kept as cold and as separated as possible, and these items need to be consumed rather quickly. Because meats are bacterial breeding grounds, I suggest they be frozen before transport, and it is imperative they be kept at the bottom and wrapped in *two* freezer bags. This will help prevent both spoilage and cross-contaminating other items in your food cooler. A thermometer should also be kept inside the cooler reading no higher than 40F and melted ice needs to be drained and replaced regularly.

Anyone who has ever hosted a kegger knows once that water starts getting warm, it has to get dumped. Otherwise, all that ends up happening is the added ice melts too quickly, and warm domestic is straight up nasty. Please do not dump your ice melt near anyone's gardens or in a water supply; you could very well introduce microbes from thawed food. It's the same reason why ice from a cooler that's storing food is never to be consumed. Camping and diarrhea do not mix well.

Dairy products, mayonnaise-based items, eggs, deli meats, refrigerated condiments and raw apple cider also need to be kept cool and consumed quickly. These should be stored above raw meats, preferably on a slotted tray or caddy. Double-wrap cheese in order to prevent cross-contamination, including melted ice. Also, do not drink straight from the container, as the cap can harbor bacteria due to the cooler's fluctuating temperatures. You're not at home. If you're really germ-conscious, use anti-bacterial wipes or even a paper towel dabbed with rubbing alcohol on such containers to help keep things clean.

Handling eggs is always tricky, but many of us cannot do without them. The easiest remedy is to bring hard-boiled eggs. They're good for salads, sandwiches, appetizers and even sliced for breakfast. But what if you want to scramble them or mix them in a recipe? You can actually freeze raw, unshelled eggs, but unlike peas, they do not have nearly the same end result. In the past, I have premixed an entire skillet breakfast before leaving home and had good results with it (not too rubbery), but I wouldn't count on being able to use that for a cake mix.

The USDA recommends using unshelled eggs within four days, so you also have the option of scrambling some up, bagging and refrigerating them in the cooler. Of course, if you just want them for scrambled eggs, why not try extra firm tofu? Mixed with veggies, tofu makes a terrific skillet breakfast with minimal effort, and the taste and texture are remarkably similar.

Anything you set out needs to maintain a consistent temperature. Wrap unused food immediately after eating and put it back in the cooler. As I mentioned before, a second, smaller cooler specifically for canned beverages will help keep the perishables from... perishing.

The cooler itself should be kept in a shady area to help prevent more ice from melting, and it should be tucked away from critters when unattended, especially at night. Raccoons and bears are keenly aware a cooler means food, and while we love our animal friends, we shouldn't be ringing the dinner bell for them. However, I do not recommend keeping the cooler in the tent during the day, because even unzipped ones tend to become saunas.

If you have the slightest bit of concern about food-borne illnesses, cook your food to an inner temperature of 180°F. Remember to keep your food *consistently* under 40°F and over 180°F are safe for three days. They say four, but I like to raise my odds. E-coli can kill you.

Vegan scraps are usually welcomed where composting is made available, but all others need to be discarded properly. Please consult your facilitator as to how food scraps are to be handled. Do not toss anything into the woods, as that invites woodland critters to dine on foods which may not be good for them. It also discourages them from eating what they should be eating, as garbage is much easier to om-nom-nom-nom on than native flora and fauna. There is also the problem of introducing non-native species to protected areas, no matter how innocuous you determine it is.

It is important to dispose of food containers properly; rinse out everything before recycling, including aluminum and freezer bags. Food scraps, and its various juices, attract animals, thanks to their keen sense of smell. (While I hate to include this when discussing food, feminine sanitary products, babies' diapers and even musty piles of clothes are all deemed delectable to critters.) If animals don't choke on your wadded up plastic wrap or cut themselves on your soup cans first, they will come into camp in search of more.

What to Do With All That Trash

At many Pagan fests, you're instructed to use the recycling bins provided and to take the rest of the trash home with you. Whah-whah-WHAT?! Many of us are so accustomed to having weekly garbage pickup that magically takes away our trash, the mere notion of being *that* responsible can seem outright absurd. Everything comes in a box, or a bag, or a jar, or more commonly, three bags in a box wrapped in a bigger box. That's A LOT of trash, and no sane urban commoner is going to want to sit with a thirty gallon garbage bag in her lap. Well, I hate to break it to ya, but if this describes you, you're about to get a crash course in living responsibly.

- I've advocated several times to consider using freezer bags for any food you prepare ahead of time, like sauces, stews and the like. They're handy, they're inexpensive, they fit well in coolers and they don't shatter. If you con't care for using plastic, there are indeed biodegradable versions of this, but they will cost you much more than you may be accustomed to spending. If the baggies are not accepted at the fest's recycling program, why not wash them out and take them home? I promise they won't take up too much space, and you'll end up saving yourself some money down the road. I know, it sounds nutty to wash little bags, but you can do it.

If that's just not going to work, there are other alternatives. While these aren't as cheap or as formidable in a cooler as the bags, I've had good experiences with plastic freezer jars. I've used mine many times over in the past year, they stack within themselves, and after several hand washings, they are still like new. The lids screw on, which keeps freezer burn out, and they come in lots of different sizes to accommodate any purpose. When you pack up to go home, they'll take up very little room, right back in the cooler you brought them with in the first place.

Of course, you can always go with the old standby of canning what you bring, but I see three pitfalls with this. For one thing, they're bulky, and a big reason why I advocate freezer bags is because you can shape them however you like before freezing. Another is because if the stuff isn't frozen, you'll rely on buying more ice (and another plastic bag from purchasing said ice) for the trip down. A third, and this should be a gimme, is traditional canning jars are made of glass. Glass breaks, especially when it's packed tightly with a bunch of heavy stuff in a moving vehicle riding over many bumps and potholes, and the jostling around of said broken glass can and will cut up nylon. The mere thought of a broken jar of spaghetti sauce or cherry pie filling has me running for the hills.

- Another major contributor of trash is paper products. Paper plates, paper towels, boxes of spaghetti... yeah, that stuff fills up a kitchen trash bag quickly at home. Many recycling systems take anything that's made of paper and cardboard, but some are rather picky about the ink on said items. Find out about the recycling rules ahead of time. Of course, using real dishes and napkins will solve a lot of these problems, and if it's okay, you can even use the rest of it as kindling for your camp's fire. Just set it aside in a dry location.

- Vegan table scraps are usually accepted for the camp's compost, but be sure it's indeed vegan. No meat, no bones, no fish (including shrimp shells), etc. Some take egg shells, and some take coffee filters, though they may request the filters and tea bags be organic, free of bleach, inks and dyes (except perhaps soy ink). If they're composting, have a little bucket nearby for collection.

- Glass, glass, glass. Some fests sort the glass, and some don't. Again, find out their recycling system ahead of time so you can plan what to bring. I shy away from anything fragile, just because I don't care for getting cut up and cleaning up messes. Anyone with a cat or a small child who decorates a tree in his home around the holidays can understand my reasoning.

- Cans, cans, cans. Soda cans. Beer cans. Tuna cans. Ravioli cans. Generally, this stuff is all made of aluminum, so this is almost universally accepted in any recycling system. Crush them down before tossing them in the buckets, unless otherwise told not to, and please rinse them out beforehand.

Why rinse them out? Well, have you ever gotten a whiff of an empty tuna can that baked in the sun for a week? Combine that smell with a hundred other cans that previously contained a wide array of prepared foods and beverages, and you have a bin with quite the aroma and "garbage juice" at the bottom. No sir, I do not want to be down wind of that. YUK! Not to mention, said juice and bits of food tends to attract all kinds of critters: Flies, maggots, raccoons, bears, bees... No thanks.

- Any camp site is sure to collect a large amount of batteries, and Pagan fests are no exception. I'm guilty of using a lot of batteries while camping, be it for my air mattress, lighting or radio, especially when it's primitive camping. I've said it before, and I'll say it again: I like to be comfortable. Battery recycling should have its own bin, if it's accepted at all. Just make sure you're tossing in the right kind in the right bin. Not all batteries are the same.

- Propane tanks and canisters have their own issues. If you use a tank, you're probably going to want to take it back with you so you can swap it out when you get back into town. However, it's the little canisters that tend to find themselves indiscriminately tossed in the trash. *Please* don't do this. Just like aerosol cans, propane canisters are dangerous and need to be handled properly. Follow the disposal directions on the can and abide by the fest's rules. If they tell you to take them home, do it.

- Some stuff like toothbrushes, deodorant containers, shampoo bottles and dish soap bottles may need to go back home with you, especially if those types of items are made with plastic. It's the rare bird indeed who uses no plastic whatsoever, but by choosing products in eco-friendly containers, even if it's only for the fest (I don't judge), it will make your drive home, and the earth breathe, easier.

- Let's face it: Murphy and his Law love to hang out at fests. Tornadoes, wandering critters, inebriated guests and everyday accidents cause damage beyond repair. For most folks, broken stuff gets tossed out and replaced, but at a fest (and at home), said broken stuff needs to have more care applied with its disposal. You may find some rather crafty Witches who will cheerfully take your ripped tarp, but odds are, you'll be bringing that back home with you. Count on it, okay?

While I again admit guilt in some of these areas, I abide by the recycling rules in order to help ensure the grounds are left even better than when I arrived. Think critically about these issues before you leave, and respect the rules while you're there. Gaia will thank you.

Staying Healthy

With all the fun and excitement going on, it can be downright hard to stay healthy while on a vacation, much less a fest. So many times, I've heard people tell me they had fallen ill, became dehydrated, came down with heat stroke or were just plain worn down. And believe me, I can most definitely understand why. While it may be more on the leisurely side of outdoor excursions, camping in and of itself can wear even the more active types of people down due to the breaking down of routine and accompanied by exposure. So before going, it's important to keep some of these (not so) common sense points in mind.

For starters, remembering the basic rules of health and wellness will go a long way. Drink, drink and drink some more... water, that is. By the time you feel thirsty, you are already dehydrated. By toting a water bottle and sipping it throughout the day, you will replenish what you sweat off just from baking in the sun, not to mention all the walking, dancing and drumming you're apt to be doing.

Even sedentary folks who stay in the shade all day still sweat, and sugary, caffeinated and/or alcoholic beverages, as delicious and refreshing as they may seem, do not do a body any favors. During the hottest parts of the day, shun the hard sweet tea and opt for plain ol' water instead. And please pay attention to the color of your urine; it should be light yellow, like lemonade. Dark urine and/or a lack of urination is a strong indicator of dehydration. If you notice this, chug away. If however you feel weak or become disoriented, immediately seek medical attention.

On that tangent, shade is your friend, as is sunblock. I am again stressing this issue, because even the best of us forget these simple rules. Additional sunblock applications are usually necessary after a dip in the stream, or after a hard rain, because the beads of water against your skin become tiny magnifying glasses for the sun's rays - even if it's an overcast day, and even if it's only 75°F. Sunglasses, hats and some type of sun blocker, even while at rest on a blanket in the grass, are vitally important for your comfort and well-being.

Eating well goes hand in hand with drinking well. Sadly, many Americans follow the SAD diet (Standard American Diet), consisting of processed foods, saturated fats, high amounts of refined sugar/high fructose corn syrup/simple carbohydrates and sodium. While at a fest, it sure can make things easy to crack open a can of spaghetti rings, stick a spoon in it and slurp it down in five minutes flat. After all, who has time to prepare, much less eat, a healthy meal when there is so much to do? And then this is expected to be done three times in any given day? *Really*?

Our bodies need routine, and that includes a routinely healthy diet. Eat what the Gods provide us and process these foods as minimally as possible. Many healthy meals can be prepared before we pack up the car and head out, and many more can be prepared at camp with only a minuscule amount of culinary know-how. I'm not saying you can't nosh on some decadent desserts after a hearty dinner; I'm the first one at the table with spoon in hand - sometimes at several campers' tables. I'm just saying to take it easy on your body so you can enjoy the fest. Five servings of fruits and vegetables should be your minimum requirement. If you can do that, you are half way there towards a healthier and happier you.

Besides eating and drinking well, and staving off the sun's rays, it's also vitally important to get enough rest. Wait, what? How is that even possible? I'm up the minute the sun starts beating down on my tent, and I tend to stay up late into the wee hours, mingling and making merry wherever I go. Even so, my body will tell me, often at the most inconvenient times, it needs to recharge. (A couple times, I completely passed out vending at a death metal concert while standing with arms crossed.) If getting in some good, honest REMs are simply not going to happen, try sipping some warm chamomile tea and relaxing in a quiet, shady spot. You just may get in the minimum forty winks your body is begging from you.

Another very important detail is to not get off schedule when taking any type of medication and to follow the prescription to the letter. Time certainly does slip away at fests, and part of it is because not too many clocks are posted. Be that as it may, the medicines designed to keep us healthy require regularity, so please remember to keep a reliable timepiece on you at all times. Many people these days rely on their cell phones for this purpose, but if you don't have a way to keep them charged for several days, you're much better off donning a wristwatch, even a cheapie digital model, possibly one that will alert you at certain times.

Also, for your sake as well as others, regular personal hygiene is more than just a strong suggestion, and some would even dare to say it's sad I have to bring this up. Body odor and bad breath aside, sometimes letting a day go without washing can seem like a no-brainer. We're on a vacation after all, and some of us feel like getting up, scooping up our toiletries and heading off to the solar showers can seem like a complete pain, especially when we're tired. Not to mention, the lines at the shower stalls can be rather long at peak times. Not everyone wants to deal with all that hot mess.

For your own health and well-being, please do not forgo this routine. Having someone check us for ticks on our backsides is more than just easing a discomfort, exfoliating keeps our largest organ, our skin, supple and moist, and practicing good oral hygiene keeps gingivitis (and more) at bay. And of course, your fellow campers will appreciate more than a token slap of patchouli oil against the skin, especially if you're the type who likes to hug.

And finally, if against all your best efforts, you do become ill, be sure to take care of yourself and not allow your sickness to fester. Stomach and other flu viruses, colds, headaches and even a tickle in your throat may need more than a pill, hot tea and a nap. Check with the festival's med center if a discomfort becomes chronic, and if you feel truly lousy, please go home. We all will indeed miss your company, but we will thank you for caring enough about our health not to pass your illness onto us and our families back home.

Dressing Up Your Campsite

> "Look around and ask yourself,
> 'Does this working environment reflect what I offer?'
> If it doesn't, then it's time to get busy."
> —Christopher Lowell

For those who have attended at least one Pagan fest, you are already fully aware just how far some of us will go to make our woodland abodes more like home. I readily admit to becoming green with envy at the ingenuity and creativity some people have devised, and that jealousy has definitely sparked some fun expressions of flair of my own. While some of what people bring with them can involve large SUVs and even separate trailers, many ideas can be implemented for the rest of us - the ones cramming as much as we can into compact cars. Let's get those creative juices flowing, shall we?

Your Tent

Think of it as more than just a roof over your head, but as a sheet of canvas (or nylon) any artist would love to paint. Acrylic paint, when coated with a spray sealant, will liven up even the grayest day. Just be sure whatever you decide to paint, you do so by going along with the color scheme you have to work with. Tying together two *un*complimentary colors is easy with a pattern; those beautiful henna designs, spirals, nature patterns, Celtic knotwork or Nordic runes are all stunning ideas.

Don't stop with the outside, as your interior should be just as inviting. I prefer using real bedding over raised air mattresses, as there is nothing better than a warm comforter and crisp sheets to rest a weary head. I also like buying my comforters a size larger than my bed, because not only does it combat the hubster from hogging it all, but it also lessens the need for a bed skirt. I also like having a cot inside not only to offer some sleeping space for others, but also as a couch and as a place to get dressed. Add a nightstand, be it inflatable or collapsible, plus a tucked away location for your clothes (under the cot perhaps?), and you'll feel right at home. And yes, I really do love my little tent ceiling fan.

Do you want something a little homier? Do an Internet search on tiny houses. I have wanted to sever ties to the land and live on the road permanently since I was a kid, but right now, it is not a possibility. But thanks to the tiny house craze, I have been looking more critically at the notion. We own a bunch of wooded acreage downstate, but we can't currently afford to move there, and we have nowhere up here to park an RV. But the portable tiny houses seem to offer the quality of living in a real home anywhere, and it wouldn't look like something to break into or drive off with (provided the wheels are hidden) while we're still stuck in the city.

Several floor plans I've seen not only would serve as an ideal home, but I could easily see myself towing it with a van to a large fest and using part of the living room as indoor merch space. I bet a few extra sales would be made just because people would want to go inside, and it would introduce folks to cool ways to live minimally. And yes, one of these modern-day vardos would certainly fit within most vendors' allotted space.

For my own tastes, I'd probably change the exterior to more of a Tudor or Chalet style, as I've always adored the dark brown X's over white paint and real window shutters. (Come to think of it, shutters would be better for the road by protecting the windows.) I'd also cover the roof with solar panels and go with all electrical appliances, perhaps even a small air conditioner. I'd also continue the loft/second floor over the front porch, as it seems silly to not make use of a few extra square feet of space.

Your "Freak" Flag

Wave it high, wave it proud. Within the confines of a fest, you may certainly do so without the neighbors looking at you funny or the association citing you with a fine. Unique covenstead flags are standards, and Jolly Rogers make regular appearances as well. Hanged plaques, without damaging any of the local flora, are equally appealing and in fact welcomes your fellow campers.

Your Kitchen and Dining Area

Obviously, I like expressing myself with the wonderful foods I create, so this is definitely my forté. Go beyond the standard mess kits and use unbreakable versions of fine china and actual silverware. You can get this stuff cheap at thrift stores, so it doesn't have to be expensive to look nice. Cloth napkins and place mats, along with a vinyl tablecloth, candles and salt and pepper shakers will transform hobo stew into an elegant feast you can't wait to savor. And, a matching towel set draped over and tied back over the camping chairs will not only provide a place for them to dry during the day, but it will add that extra bit of *style* any design magazine would be proud to feature.

Your Rec Space

After the dishes have been cleared, it's time to party. Tiny solar LED lights are now available, which you can weave into your canopy shelter and help liven the mood. (And yes, you may want to paint your canopy as well.) Just remember *condensa-*

tion will kick in after dusk, so your drums will need to be tightened, your playing cards will dampen and curl, and your tablecloth will collect little puddles of dew. By hanging onto your place mats, and use an extra one for the ante pot, you'll be able to stave off most of these problems.

Something I have wanted to do for ages is to set up a camping version of a suburban back yard. Those little picket fences people use for gardening would look so adorable, paired with an inflatable kiddie pool. On a scorching hot summer day, you just *know* you're going to have a lot of company. Throw some dogs and burgers on the grill, mix up some cool drinks in your outdoor kitchen, and viola - Instant party.

Your Powder Room

Instead of relying on the privvies and public shower stalls, many people opt to bring their own. It sure makes the trek shorter in the middle of the night, and yes, basic human functions can retain a bit more privacy. Feel free to decorate this shelter like the others, and set up even a small table for your toiletry needs. A hand mirror and a wash basin will make any campsite feel more like home.

Your Vending/Workshop Area

Since many vendors work in front of or beside their campsites, see if you can tie the theme together. Paint your vending tent, weave in some lights (which will help evening shoppers see your wares), sell some of your plaques and flags, and wave hello while sipping from an unbreakable margarita glass. Hmmm... this really doesn't seem like work at all anymore - talk about your working vacations.

A Guide to Pagan Camping

To utilize the *literal* notion of tying things together, use the same brightly-colored string or duct tape on all of your lines. This is definitely a case of form *and* function here, preventing people from tripping over your lines and crashing into your tent while adding some extra flair to your woodland abode.

Another option for marking lines I've seen in the past are using those small solar light stakes. They run about $2 a piece, and they will certainly clue people in on where to step. I however do not recommend using too many, as not only will the bright LED lights garner some unwanted attention from the soft lighting advocates, but when set up in straight lines, your site will look more like an airport than a campsite, on top of attracting extra bugs.

A third option I've seen is rather English cottage charming. Consider disguising the lines with silk flowers, ivy and even little bells and other sparkly, dangly things, which will serve as tiny wind chimes. Just be sure whatever you use has hints of bright colors and/or is reflective, because you still need to have your decorations serve its primary function.

However you decide to set up your campsite, be sure to do it with your personality and your spirituality reflected. Not only will you get more out of your retreat, but you will be adding your magic to the community that has welcomed you.

Playing Nice in the Sandbox

"The best subjects are always people, who never fail to amaze me by their unpredictability."
—Ronnie James Dio

With so many different types of people getting together, heads are bound to butt. I prefer to pull the old standby of the nod and smile when it comes to people with whom I (vehemently) disagree, but that's a lot easier to say than do when they're all up in your business. And what's worse, by choosing not to contribute to a (volatile) topic, you can still be misconstrued, even though the only thing you want is to get back to enjoying the fest.

What's this Witch to do? It's not like I'm going to pack up and go home just because Lord Greenie McEarthyPants called me out for using my trusty freezer bags and wearing shoes made in China. I'll just ignore him, even though I can see him talking about me with his pointing gestures, making my blood boil.

I'm also not going to kowtow to Her High Priestess Aradia-Fae MoonStorm, even though she declared my wares toxic and belong in a red light district. She wonders how I was even permitted to attend and then will go on to publicly state anyone who shops at my booth supports misogyny, homophobia, racism and a slew of other nasty, scary categories.

Wait, *what?* Where did all of *that* come from? Suddenly, without really doing anything other than just sitting there eating lunch, I find myself a target... or maybe it's all in my head. Did Greenie really just call me out, or did he merely make a suggestion? He *did* have a bit of a tone, but meh... I'll just let him ramble. He'll eventually find someone else to talk ~~to~~ *at*.

As for Ms Longname, I have to wonder if she would declare such things if she were to only read the lyrics. But I have a feeling that isn't going to make her happy. So, I'll interrupt her mid-sentence and inquire where she got that intricate necklace.

Even if you're at a smaller fest where you don't have too many places to run away from the nutjobs, bullies and grand-standers, here's my suggestion: refuse - defuse - confuse.

Refuse: This is my favorite tactic, following Mom's advice of not saying anything. By refusing to contribute or otherwise become a part of someone's craziness, just nodding and smiling, a good portion of these types of people will eventually go away. It's been my experience the only types of people who will continue to talk *at* me when I'm obviously not interested are drunk.

Defuse: When I feel personally attacked, my first reaction is to defend myself and fight back. "Oh no she didn't!" I believe is the commonly accepted expression. But am I really going to jump from behind the table and tackle some svelte twenty-something who thinks my jeans are too tight? No, because this isn't an action movie, and I'm not Ahh-nald.

However, I may be tempted to verbally do something similar, thinking I'm being witty. Nope, I'm probably going to come off as being petty instead, or most likely, a horse's ass. I'll just state I try to be healthy, and I eat a wide variety of foods, but y'know, I like sugar. A lot. That will probably lead her to ramble on and on about all the things she does to be better than me, which will eventually have her talking *at* me, which will lead to her getting bored and finding someone else to correct or whatever.

Confuse: One of my new favorite tactics on the message boards that gives assholes the hint they're indeed being assholes is to respond to their ridiculous rants with "I like turtles". (It works for a lot of things really, but it's my favorite reply to assholes.) I used a variant of that once on an online customer who was being nonsensical, and he eventually went away, realizing his long-winded complaints were falling on deaf ears and was not even paying any attention to him. See ya.

Completely blind-siding an asshole, or a complainer, or some high and mighty Grand Poobah grand-stander in a positive way can actually switch gears so strongly you just may make a new friend. Crazier things have happened. Ms. Longname has an agenda: in an effort to serve her many causes, she seeks out the Boogie Man around every corner, and by doing so, she gains an even stronger alliance.

By commenting on her gorgeous necklace, she may pause for a moment and say, "Oh this?" I image she would momentarily forget her staunch objections and go on to describe, in great detail, how Ms. Even*Longer*Name made it especially for her and gave it to her in an elaborate pomp and circumstance that may as well been telecast over Charles and Diana's wedding.

Of course, because she's such an important person, she will be called away at some point during her stories, but with her parting your company on a high note. After all, almost every Big Name Pagan I've ever met has an ego that likes stroking, because let's face it, most creative and expressive people are hard-wired that way. Am I guilty of this? You bet. And sometimes, I need to be put in check as well. So there ya go.

Just remember, the point of going to a fest is to build a Pagan community, and every community has people whose opinions differ from your own. If you can't find a commonality, then just let it go. So may Witch Wars have carried on over years and even decades, and many times, it's over stupidity.

Sexuality and Pagan Festivals

> *"Let my worship be within the heart that rejoiceth, for behold: all acts of love and pleasure are my rituals."*
> —Doreen Valiente, <u>The Charge of the Goddess</u>

This is a pretty important topic to cover, one I almost decided to dedicate a chapter to, as nudity, sex and many Pagan fests can indeed be symbiotic by nature. I am a rather shy person, some may even say prudish, when it comes to sexuality, but because many of our various and collective faiths promote even understood degrees of fertility, I tend to be open-minded on the subject. After all, where would we be if our biological parents hadn't joined?

The problem lies primarily due to our upbringings as well as what societal norms dictate. At a fest where clothing is an option rather than a requirement, some people get it in their heads none of the standard rules apply. Well, yes indeed they do, because while we are allowed to express ourselves through our bodies, we are still held to a high degree of standards in making such expressions.

The hard and fast rules (no pun intended) are to acknowledge each person's Will and to honor their choices. Some people are like me and do not even like seeing themselves nude in a mirror, and some people wish society would allow them to pick up the newspaper on their doorsteps without first tying on a robe. Both positions should be acknowledged as well as honored.

At such fests, if you happen to notice someone completely nude whipping up breakfast, it may at first seem rather jarring. Acknowledge that person is just doing what feels right and natural and move on if it truly bothers you. Trust me, you'll eventually get used to it, and when you do, you'll feel a bit more comfortable walking by and waving hello. When it comes to honoring other people's natural choices, that does not mean you have to *dis*honor your own or make yourself feel uncomfortable in any way.

I must stress you are not required to participate in any situations that make you uncomfortable. If you believe full or partial nudity will temporarily blind you or is simply inappropriate for you or members of your group, there are some fests you may wish to skip. Be sure to investigate if the fest you're considering attending has only certain areas where the clothing option exists, and whether or not that will include the main ritual, workshops you'd like to attend, the vending and showering areas and during the potluck feast. Segregated fests are out there, but be aware that does not mean you won't catch a glimpse of anything from a distance.

At fests, one can usually attend workshops centered around, or focused on, sex and sexuality. If they pique your interest, be sure to investigate. As with anything else in life, there is always room for growth. (Again, no pun intended.) Be sure to learn beforehand if there will be any topics or media presented that you feel will make you uncomfortable. You can (anonymously) ask around if anyone has ever attended one of these workshops or knows the presenter and her style. If this sounds good to you – go. There are just some topics that are better absorbed through workshops than reading material. And yes, share what you learn with willing participants if you like. What's the fun in learning or honing a skill if you keep it to yourself?

Pagan fests are indeed liberating, but this can cause various degrees of miscommunication. While you are certainly under no obligation to perform the Great Rite with anyone who asks, don't be surprised if you are invited to participate. This includes me, the happily monogamous lady, who does take offense to such invites from people who have already made well aware of my position. While I'm not surprised, and I do admire persistence in the general sense, this should be common sense stuff. No means no. It does not mean not right now. It does not mean to let me think it over. And it most certainly does not mean yes. Be on the prowl all you want, but don't be surprised when your lack of subtlety gets you shot down and perhaps even slapped... several times.

It should go without saying, but there is no such thing as pleading ignorant. "Fifteen gets you twenty", as the saying goes, and consensual sex with a minor *is not* consensual: it's called statutory rape. When I was a teen, I was often mistaken for being over eighteen by people who didn't know me, innocuous or otherwise. At thirteen, I was a professional model: I had slinky curves and large breasts, I wore makeup, and my round yet thin face disguised my youth.

As I got older, the tell-tale signs became even harder to distinguish, which worked in my favor when I wanted to gain entry to certain events and clubs. Of course, that was back in the 80s when most bouncers and clerks didn't ask for identification from everyone under forty. They ask now, because they do not want to risk prosecution due to heavy laws set in place, and because it's the right thing to do. Therefore, you should follow their lead.

Should you have (or find) a willing partner or two, it is important to consider the results of such encounters. An elder once jokingly wondered out loud how many children she noticed in attendance had begun their lives *at* that fest. Sex is a joyous part of our humanity, and it should be celebrated. But as an adult, much less one who practices a fertility religion, you should already know sexual intercourse can and does tend to result in babies.

Children are indeed our future and are beautiful, innocent and unconditionally loving. A good portion of us were not planned, but most of our caregivers took on the task of raising us, even if we may now feel they could have done (much?) better. Children are a great responsibility that can push us to our limits of sanity and financial hardship, with women finding themselves throughout history bearing the brunt of it. So while we may feel we have dropped the shackles of such oppressions through hard work and modern science, being prepared for babies can result from any such coupling, even with precautions taken. Fests are intended to create community, but that doesn't mean you have to start your own.

Even if you two, or three, or more, avoid that particular aspect of exploring your sexuality, precautions again need to be taken. Diseases are no joke, and unless you know your partner(s) well, condoms are a necessity rather than an option. If you have even an inkling you may opt to engage in sex with people you passively know, and you most certainly can with willing partner(s), bring your own condoms - men and women alike. Choose a brand that adds an extra *Oomph!* to your passion but also prevents diseases. It's also imperative to learn if you are allergic to latex, if you do not already know. Never assume someone else will "spot you" or even cares about your health. In the 21st century, this should all be common sense, but hey, our passions can overcome our other senses.

Now yes, we're all adults here, but there are those of us, me included, who stroke our inner ego - liberally and often. (Okay, yes, *that* pun was definitely intended.) Laughter and joy are good medicine, and sometimes, it comes out at the most inconvenient times. If your passion is loudly expressed, even within the confines of your tent (which is constructed of canvas or nylon rather than brick and mortar), don't be surprised if people walk by with saucy smirks. "*Day no whut u did dare.*" Meh, they probably did, too. Just keep in mind the occasional lapse in retention is funny, but such recurring expressions are usually considered annoying by most. And for some of us involuntary listeners, that's just straight up showing off. Hey, I callz 'em like I seez 'em.

Remember, fests are designed to express yourselves and invoke closeness and communication. It is how any community is built. How close you choose to get to know others is your choice alone, and no one should ever force that upon you. If something <u>ever</u> feels wrong to you, do not ever hesitate to say no. If you are attacked, and sadly fests are not completely immune to such behavior (but are blessedly extremely rare), please report this to the authorities. Don't ever feel ashamed. You said *no* or were unable to say *yes*. It's not your fault.

I'm sure there are other aspects of this important topic left to cover, and I invite you to add your insight. I want to end on a high note, because for me, sex at fests is some of the best I've ever had, and I really do not want to ever discourage anyone from exploring. "Vacation sex" generally is awesome, (except for that one time we can laugh about *now*), because you're in a new environment and don't have home matters to worry about. That loosens your inhibitions and allows you to be free. Relish it, cherish it, embrace it for all its worth, but please do so respectfully and responsibly.

Building Community through Your Gifts and Talents

> *"The community which has neither poverty nor riches will always have the noblest principles."*
>
> —Plato

For people who've never attended a Pagan festival before, seeing the work shift section on the application could send some folks seething. Believe me, I get it, because this is not the way many secular/mundane events are handled. Normally, you pay a fee, you arrive, you set up, you do your thing and you leave. Everything else is provided for you. Working *in addition to* paying can most certainly come off as a foreign notion. You may even be thinking the work shift part is some kind of encouraged discount, that you can just pay more if you want. While some fests do allow that, the work shift is actually an integral part of the fest. Allow me to explain the why's.

First off, having everyone pitch in a bit does indeed defer labor costs. One of my ultimate pilgrimages on the mundane level is the Wacken Open Air festival. (Yes, in case you didn't know, I'm a major Metal Chick.) In addition to the costs of just getting to Germany, I'm well aware my admission fee is going to be rather high for three days of hedonistic fun. That's because the WOA folks will be supplying me with space to camp, lots of great music (including labor and set-up), security and even a seemingly impromptu grocery store. Managing that many people, as well as the messes and situations they create (especially when infused with libations) is expected to cost a pretty penny. So, when a Pagan festival, which is not managed or even monetarily assisted with corporate sponsorship, opts to include work shifts, you can see how this is sensible.

So okay, they're working on a shoestring budget, so forced volunteerism simply makes sense. Well, it's not really the main reason. I just listed it first, because I wanted to plead to your common sense. The *real* reason behind work shifts is to truly build a community, albeit a temporary one. Just like in "the real world", everyone has a job to do in order to make things happen. Somebody has to police your town, somebody has to clean up the streets, somebody has to build the houses, somebody has to sell things we want and need, somebody has to broadcast the news, and somebody has to provide the entertainment and classes.

If *you* do this for your new community, then you don't have to rely on some stranger to do it, who many or may not "get you". Think about it: Don't you wish your town had Pagans running things, even as a fleeting fantasy? Even if you're a hardcore Thelemite, and the sales clerks look like "fluffy bunnies" running around in Birkenstocks and tie-dyed sarongs, smelling of patchouli and thanking your patronage with a "*Namaste*", at least they "get you" and won't judge your beliefs or strange attire (or lack thereof).

And on that tangent, having the community put in their time keeps things cool. Some people who attend are still "in the broom closet" and don't want people outside the community to know how they spend their off time. In 2004, the Pagan Spirit Gathering was invaded by a news crew who tried to get the dish on what was going on. While it seems most people found the event entertaining to have a news helicopter flying overhead, I'm sure those who want to keep their *private* lives private found it to be an unwelcome experience... to say the least.

To me, the whole thing reeked of paparazzi ~~journalism~~ sensationalism. I know a lot of folks in my local community who hide their religious beliefs for various reasons: Jobs, custody battles, bigoted neighbors, etc., and justifiably so. It's not easy to be as open as I am, but then again, I've never been a shrinking violet, and I am willing and able to handle any extra attention my beliefs and views create. I'm *Metal like that*, as a friend once said. But hey, I'm not everyone else; as I said before, I get it.

Getting back to the reasons, we've already covered the financial, and we've touched upon the community-building and security. But really, besides people working there who "get you", the most important reason to cheerfully contribute via work shifts is to actually become an integral part of the festival itself. When you check people in, you meet a lot of people, and you can figure out who you may want to get to know better. When you go hoarse from running around and letting people know the next workshop is starting, you become a vital piece of information. When you play with the kids, you get to know their parents who just may invite you over for supper. And when you perform, you forge a more permanent and die-hard fan base. You make friends you'll never forget, you learn how to do new things for yourself, and you bring back to your nine to five a renewed sense of belonging to a community that may have only been in the virtual beforehand. You become One.

So yes, think about what work shift you'd like to do and are good at doing, and do so willingly and on time. (Pagan Standard Time doesn't do anyone any favors.) The work you do is *for* you as much as it is for everyone else, and no matter how insignificant you feel your contribution is, it's not. And, it's appreciated.

Work Shift with the Kids

Since everyone is required to do a work shift or two at many Pagan festivals, some may think "babysitting" during their shift(s) is easy. After all, it wasn't all that hard to do back in high school, right? Click on the TV, get some homework done, raid the fridge and yap on the phone. Done and done.

Uhhhh... no. You're expected to do a lot more than that. One of my fondest memories in the community is when I ran the kids' room at a hotel convention some years back. I specifically did not want it to be a dump-off location so the parents could attend the various workshops; I wanted the kids to feel welcomed and an integral part of the convention. The way I see it, our kids are indeed our future, and it is our job to gently guide them without stepping on their parents' toes.

Since the convention _(Ancient Ways in Chicago)_ was held the three-day weekend after Thanksgiving, the upcoming holiday was Yule. So, I went with that general theme and ran with it. My thinking was who doesn't like Yule?! There's that, and I also figured it was a safe theme to use, since most children revere Santa, even if they're not raised in Pagan homes.

So, I brought in our artificial tree and some lights from home and set it up, asking the kids to help me create ornaments for it and to decorate the room. I supplied many bottles of glue, safety scissors, glitter, printer and construction paper, scented pine cones, crayons, yarn, Popsicle sticks, masking tape, cotton balls and pipe cleaners out of my own pocket. I also dragged in my traveling library of kids' books our son had outgrown (that I have since passed on to the local homeschool group.) I had the hotel supply me with a folding table and chairs, and for that, I also brought in a spool of vinyl table cloth from a party store, in order to save the convention folks clean-up costs, like glue getting spilled on the carpeting. (Ya know that was bound to happen.)

With the kids, I sat down and began working on all kinds of projects. By me sitting there and doing the projects along with them, they saw it was fun to do, and they could ask me questions in an easy-going environment. Any religious talk that came about, I remembered to keep it as neutral as possible or to reiterate this is what I believe. We made sparkly pine cone ornaments, snowflakes, paper chains, cards... you name it. By the end of the convention, before the kids came back to collect their projects, that boring, stuffy convention room was, without a doubt, right up there in competition with Will Ferrel's elven rendition welcoming Santa at the department store.

Because I knew the kids would be coming and going throughout the day, wanted to have the room as inviting as possible and to meet as many interests and ages as well. For that, I also had the AV department supply me with a TV/DVD combo and ran videos. I posted a decorative sign outside, stating when each DVD would be played and its rating. Between showings, I played a children's holiday CD on my boom box. (And no, I surprisingly did *not* get sick of that chipmunk whining about wanting a hula hoop.) I even created a photocopied coloring storybook I both wrote and illustrated, with a couple simple recipes included, just so the kids would have a keepsake.

Because I had put in a lot of my own time and money into making the kids' room an awesome place, I felt no shame in putting out a donation basket, which I started off with some pocket change and a dollar. I distinctly remember the little card I wrote next to it, because I still pat myself on the back for being direct, tactful, witty *and* cute:

> *Books and crafts cost money,*
> *DVD's do, too.*
> *Won't you be so kind,*
> *As to drop a buck or two?*

Naturally, I didn't recover all my costs, but I actually came pretty close to breaking even. Then again, I've always been a smart shopper, and I've been buying up some of that stuff over a couple months as I came across a sale. There's that, and because I also ran the local Pagan family group, some of that stuff I already had on hand or figured it would be used down the road.

It's been quite a few years since that convention, but it warms my heart to hear from so many parents who still thank me for going all out to make the kids feel welcome. And yep, they still have the ornaments on their family trees. I feel so special to know I made that much of an impact, when I really did was have fun playing with the kids. It did not feel like work at all.

I know this sounds *waaaaay* above and beyond the average one to two hour work shift, but I just wanted to illustrate how far one could take it. Most of what I did was planned ahead of time with open-ended projects, allowing the fun to grow organically. If you ask me, working with the kids in our community is way more fun and rewarding than handling a lot of the adult-oriented workshops, because kids don't have as many preconceived notions or expectations.

As long as the children followed a basic list of rules, I extended to them the attention and respect they gave to me. And that set of rules - I had it prominently placed on the open door (whenever I was available), just so parents can slyly check in or even join in on the fun. As a parent, the thought of a complete stranger with my son in a closed room would never have sat well.

Presenting a Pagan Workshop

As I've already discussed, most festivals require you to put in time toward the community via work shifts. In many cases, you can opt to do a presentation or workshop instead of "grunt work". If you are interested in doing something a little more creative, read on.

First of all, you should already be familiar with these. If you've never attended one, even at an indoor convention or one-day holiday event, I highly suggest you do so. Take in at least three, because you want to get a gauge on different styles for running one. Be sure to take lots of notes on what you liked best about each presenter's style, where you think they could have done better, and whether or not the group appeared to have gotten a lot out of it. (You'll probably find that out afterward in the hallway, based upon how much people talk amongst themselves.)

Most of the time, these are done in classroom-style settings, where the presenter (you) would be explaining your topic to a group of people. Depending on your topic of (niche) expertise, this may be the easiest way to go. The most dynamic workshops I've ever attended included various uses of media: discussion, worksheets, music, slides/film/photographs and lots of questions and answers before, during and when wrapping things up

Notice too I used the word *niche*. No doubt, there will be workshops based around "Wicca 101"-type topics, but those are typically reserved for well-known authors/BNPs (Big name Pagans), if they're presented at all. And if so, they probably will also be covering the 102's, 201's and so forth, along with plugging their latest book. Therefore, if your idea was to do a presentation on setting up an altar, blessing a candle or charging a wand, you will want to consider another one.

Think critically:

- What do you do differently than recommended by the most popular Pagan/Wiccan books?
- If you are decidedly not Wiccan, Neo-Wiccan, Eclectic Wiccan or anything having to do with Wicca whatsoever, do you feel you have practiced your faith long enough to offer a glimpse into it?
- Do you feel the current workshops and books based on your faith *only* provide such glimpses, and you feel you can certainly go more deeply into it?
- How do you already serve your local community you feel others would like to learn more about?
- What meditation style works best for you that you came up with yourself?
- What accomplishment have you made that has bettered your local, or even global, community?

If you have answered "Yes" to any of these questions, or if you have a topic beyond the ones I listed, then I answer you back with another "Yes!" - you probably *should* consider doing a workshop. We need your wisdom and experience.

Now again, if you've never presented a workshop before, you may feel intimidated about doing so. About ten years ago, my first formal presentation was done at the Chicago Pagan Expo. My topic was on Pagan parenting, which I was actually invited to do, since I had begun organizing family-oriented events in the community. I was Scared. To. Death. I remember the hour before my slot, my palms were so sweaty I bled through my top index card. I had to write a new one, because the ink had smeared all over the place. But by the time people started walking in, I began to calm down a bit, and the vibe in the room lightened up as well.

At that point, I began the workshop by thanking everyone for coming and taking time out of their day. I handed out a scrapbook of all the fun events our kids have done, which I asked folks to pass around. I also distributed booklets detailing what it is we did, with contact information included.

While the scrapbook made its rounds, I went into detail on the most recent event we held for the kids: The Ostara egg hunt. As the guests flipped through the pictures, I pointed out how the kids handled the bulk of the ritual and how the community helped ensure such a wonderful event. That was the key to the bulk of my workshop, the whole *it takes a village* notion. And from there, we wrapped up with some Q and A, which led into a good deal of discussion.

Was my presentation successful? I believe it was, as people asked me further questions afterward. Soon after that, our little group gained quite a few new members, which led to more activities and lots of online chatter. And, after that first time speaking in front of the community, which for me is *unlike* the classroom public speaking (even in college), I was that much more willing to do so down the road.

Now in my case, the tone I wanted to set was fun, playful and exciting, because hanging out with the kids is just that. Were I to address a group about domestic violence in the community, the tone I'd set would be drastically different. I didn't have a projector or even a laptop back then to illustrate my discussion, but if I did, I would have definitely utilized that by playing some video footage, or blowing up the photographs, or anything else I could think of. With your topic in mind, what tools would *you* use to enliven your workshop?

Now that you know what you'd like to do, you'll need to submit it to the fest facilitators for their approval. Detail what you plan on doing, what tools you will be using, how long it will be and of course, why you feel your workshop would benefit the community. If you can, provide two, three or even more submissions, just in case your first choice is denied or is too similar to another workshop already scheduled. Be sure to attach your outlines to the form supplied, dot your I's and cross your T's, and send them either by email with a reply request or via certified mail. After that, the wonderful world of waiting begins... (Don't you love that?)

If your submission is accepted, you need need to plan out everything you said you were going to do. If you'll be promoting something, be sure to include that someplace prominently but without being pushy - coming off as a used car salesman. You may be able to do this at your booth, which would be rather convenient, as you would be easily able to point out where your group could purchase or learn more about whatever it is you're promoting. Tact goes a long way here.

After all your prep work, try out your presentation on a couple friends. Listen to their constructive criticisms closely, because while these folks know you personally, your group will not. If they tell you it's too dry, ask them how you can make it more lively. If they say you're talking too fast, learn how to pace yourself. (*Breathe... breathe.*) And, if the worksheet(s) you provided are confusing, have your friends make notes on how to clarify things.

Keep in mind body language accounts for a good portion of your presentation, so dress appropriately, open your arms, speak freely and *smile*. Think of your group as guests in your home.

You wouldn't stand in attention with your arms crossed, only opening them to check your watch every five minutes to see when they'll be leaving. No way! Nor would you be using every twenty five cent word you could muster while chatting over tea. Unless you are addressing a serious issue and reading from a script, you should be speaking freely and from the heart.

If your friends give you a big thumbs up, you should be ready to go. Just remember to pack any tools you need to liven things up, as well as to provide some type of business card in case folks would like to get a hold of you after the fest. They don't need to be fancy, but they should be more than torn off slips of paper. Photocopied brochures are rather easy and inexpensive to create, and people can follow along the bullet points while you delve into your discussion. But above all, love what you do. This is your baby - run with it.

Musical Performances

Doing a gig at a Pagan fest is a bit different than performing at Flapjack McGillicuddy's Bar and Grill, the Willow Tree County Fair or even SuperMegaCorporateName Arena. As a record producer, my husband and I have have had numerous and unique privileges of experiencing just what our bands go through to bring their craft to the people who love their work. (And too, the hubster went through these same experiences as a musician himself.) Yes, some of the scene is indeed glamorous-fabulous, but sometimes too, it is downright painful. Pagan fests are rarely ever on the *painful* side, and they are very much in a class all their own.

Most of the time, as you well know, a gig is someplace in-between, yet no matter where we are, it's the place to be. When it comes to Pagan fests specifically, I often admire the facilitators for doing such a bang-up job to make sure the entertainment part runs so smoothly, on top of everything else they do. (I love you, man.) Just by putting together several one-day events over the years, I know how many months of planning that entails. Therefore, I can't even remotely fathom how much harder it is to do the magic they do, and do it with a smile and not even appearing to break a sweat.

Most Pagan fests our bands have worked with operate on standard industry professionalism. You find out who to contact, you send in their desired format of a press kit (everybody's different these days), you wait for your answer and you go from there. Many bands invited are asked to perform as free entry and merch vending, travel pay or something more substantial, so your acceptance depends on quite a number of things. Please consider:

- Fest history
- Equipment provided
- Who's handling the promotion
- How well it will be promoted
- Which bands will be headlining
- Which slot can be guaranteed
- Where gear will be stored
- Expected attendance
- Goal of performance

On our end (us and the bands we represent), we attend as many different types of music fests as possible, because not only do we go to see the shows themselves, we consider them partly as trade conventions. For our bands with a Pagan slant, we of course primarily attend to give back to the community that's taken good care of us, but we also hope the community will reciprocate with applause and perhaps even a CD purchase or two.

The larger fests operate with the utmost experienced professionalism, albeit on a tighter budget than you may be accustomed. There will be a large stage with a giant fest backdrop, pro gear powered by a great sound guy, stellar lighting and everything is run right on schedule. Not to mention, when you arrive, you're greeted by a swath of fans all vying for your attention, thanks to the tremendous amount of promotion and hyping. Yep, this is going to be one for the record books.

Many others though are being run by folks who genuinely love their faith and community and have hearts of gold. But (and you saw this coming), they really don't know too much about running a fest other than printing a few fliers and sending out some emails. That's okay - not a problem - just let them know the minimums you can work with and see how you can make the fest a real success. After all, they do have their hearts in the right place, and who knows - this little gathering may very well become the next Starwood or even a Burning Man. You/your band stand the same chance of becoming an A-Lister yourselves, so why not help this little fest grow? Besides, it's been said some of the best shows are the smallest, because the fans *all* came to see you play. They tell two friends, and *they* tell two friends, and *they* tell two friends...

One fest one of our bands performed at a couple times was in Michigan, just on the other side of the lake from here in Chicago. The facilitator started it, as he owned a huge amount of land and envisioned offering that land as a gathering of the (younger) tribes who wanted more of a variety than the traditional folksy standbys. He didn't have a whole lot of experience at that level, and yes, there were some snafus only an outdoor fest could create (damn you Murphy and your Law). But, these snafus were minor and handled very well by diligent and attentive volunteers. No big deal - everyone had a great time, and the show itself was worth it.

One of the snafus I wanted to mention is our collective pet peeve: *condensation.* When the headlining act performed, they experienced this first hand more than anyone else, as they played after the moisture started rising from the grass. While we as audience members didn't notice too much, as we were busy enjoying the show, they did. Everything was going out of tune, so it made it rather hard for them to play. I mention this so you can be prepared to handle condensation if you never have before. I tell bands all the time to just keep playing, because again, wherever you are, it's the place to be. Send out those positive vibes and all that.

Also, since the fest itself was still in its budding phase, the equipment was all run by generators, and generators need to be periodically fed with gasoline. So yeah, all the bands shared in at least one case of an "intermittent intermission", depending on how much electricity and how long of sets they had. However, none of the performers really cared about the little dings, because this was not just a show - this was a Pagan fest. We've huddled together through thunderstorms, tornadoes, bears - we can certainly handle a little dampness and spontaneous mead and beer run breaks.

Now true, I am indeed advocating to "cut the (new) guys some slack" here, because budding Pagan fests are serving our community and not funding some corporate huckster's boat payments. However, giving back does not mean you should just let everything business-like go on the wayside. You're still a professional here, so you should keep things professional - albeit a bit friendlier.

My biggest suggestion to any performer, no matter where she plays, is to get it all in writing. Any fest should provide you with a run-down of everything included in an itinerary, even if it's in email format. Go through the list previously mentioned, especially how the fest will be promoted (radio, flyers, ads, emails, blog postings, etc.). After all, what good will it do to load up your trailer and drive half way across the country to play if no one will show up?

You'll also want to know if the fest is going to be fully insured, where you'll be parking, your load-in time, whether or not you're expected to be there for the entire duration, where and when you can vend and if they'll feed you that night or any other time. Always email the facilitator any dialog you exchange, so you will have proof of what was said and agreed upon, as well as any updates or changes being made as time progresses.

And, because these fests *do* operate a bit differently, you're probably going to need to pack a bit heavier than usual. Yup, that means bringing along some camping gear, even if you've made arrangements to crash in someone's tent. (Remember, mosquito repellent is your friend.) As I've stated before, the whole idea is to build community, and usually the performers are expected to hang around at least a night. I know you may have been planning to make it to another show the next night that's six hours away, but instead of packing up and staying at a hotel (or driving straight through), why not camp out with your fans? It's fun, and that's the whole point of being a performer - to love what you do. Believe me, it's certainly not to strike it rich. Leave that to the fairytale stories promoted on music-based documentaries… errr reality shows.

If you stay, and you should, you'll have a huge opportunity to sell and sign CDs, as you have a captive audience so to speak. Be sure to bring your long sleeves and knit caps, because it gets chilly at night and fans *will* buy them. Not to mention, your fans are going to treat you like gold and shower you with attention and affection. You're a Rawk Stah after all, but more importantly, you're showing your fans you're real people, one of them in spirit and faith, and you're good friends worth knowing. By spending at least a night, you've just solidified a die-hard batch of fans who will follow you until you're old and gray, through thick and thin. The power of kinship and camaraderie never cease to amaze me.

As you can see, Pagan fests are not your ordinary gigs, but they are certainly always worth playing. They're good for your spirit, and the fans are some of the most dedicated people I've ever had the pleasure to meet.

Festival Vending

Several years of running a record label has provided my husband and I with quite a bit of vending experience, both in and outdoors. Please allow me to break it down for you:

1. <u>Never</u> vend alone - bring a buddy. Ron and I are successful, because there are at least two of us running the booth. This allows us to trade off watching the table while the other makes a dash to the privvies, gets some food, check out a performance or presentation, plus it guarantees someone is always watching our stuff. Theft is fairly unlikely, especially at Pagan festivals, but don't assume everyone follows that code of ethics.

2. Always pick a spot *away* from the major drumming areas and loud presentations, but close enough to be seen from those same areas. Most of what you're selling is <u>you</u>, not your products, so you need to be far enough away to be able to talk to your customers. Also, get an idea where the most amount of people are going to congregate to view the performance, and allow yourself a safe distance. People who drink a lot have a tendency to crash into whatever is near them, including your booth. Another great spot, if all the good ones are taken, is near the privvies. Everyone has to answer the call of nature at some point in time. Just be sure you're down-wind.

3. Set up your booth right after you set up your tent, and you should <u>always</u> get there early. Most of your selling will occur during the day, when people first get there, when the cash is burning a hole in their pockets. We've seen *sooo* many bands and other vendors lose out on sales, because they set up after the majority of people have already made the bulk of their purchases. We stay open until the last performance of the evening, or when it becomes obvious people are no longer interested in shopping with anyone (which is usually when it's pitch-black and people are starting to pass out just any ole place.)

4. Be aware sales will slump during major acts and presentations, but people will still wander, so always be on the ready. And for Gods' sakes, do not sit there looking bored. It gives the impression you're not having a good time and could care less about being there in the first place. Craft jewelry, reorganize your goods, check your inventory – whatever.

If it's a major down-time, look busy and *smile*. Reading the paper or napping is *not* the impression you want to be sending out. If you need some time away because your ass is getting sore, your ears are starting to ring or you just want a good stretch, that's what your buddy is there for.

5. This always happens to us, so I think this is a good time to mention this. Merchants need to eat just like everyone else, but please don't continue to munch while customers are present. If you sneak away to grab a sandwich and a customer showed up just as you were about to take a bite, go ahead and take that bite but put the food down. Say something funny like,

"Ack! Ya caught me!" Tuck the food away and wipe your mouth and hands. Just as napping and reading give off an uninviting impression, so does chowing down on lunch. You can't answer a question when you have food stuffed in your mouth. Sorry, but you'll just have to wait a little bit longer, because your job is to give the customer her undivided attention.

6. Have an ashtray and a garbage can next to your booth, and have some paper towels or a rag on hand. Smokers are constantly on the lookout to butt out their cigarettes, and if you have an ashtray, they just might make a double-take at your booth. Even if you're hugely against smoking, you're making an effort to prevent litter by providing such a vessel, perhaps crafted out of a soda can and fused to the table with duct tape.

When people shop, they need both hands, so they need to have a space to set down their drink. Save a *small* space for that, perhaps even labeling it as such. Having something to wipe down the condensation (and small spills) from their drinks prevents your table from getting ruined, including the stuff on it. NOT offering this to people has them wander elsewhere, plus it can make it appear you're either highly judgmental or not the happiest of hosts of your rural abode.

7. Provide lots of light for people to shop. It gets awful dark at night, so keep that in mind. Besides moths, lights *also* attract people to your booth over a dark booth. A good idea is also to have a flashlight available for customers' use, allowing them to focus in on small details, since some people's night vision is just plain bad. This goes for indoor vending as well, because venues turn all the lights off, except for the stage itself. Be creative with the lighting, using scented candles, on top of lanterns and such, and have the lights facing *away* from your customers as much as possible. No one enjoys being blinded.

8. When the sun sets, bugs love your lanterns. Try to keep them away from your merch as much as possible. We have a vending tent that we can hook the lantern on top, allowing the critters to fly merrily around overhead (similar pictured), instead of flailing all over the table. That makes for a very uncomfortable visit at your station (not to mention, it's just plain gross.)

9. Speaking of merch tents, to Hell with the screened-in ones. They're a bitch to set up, and they keep more bugs in than out. Find one that works like the chairs (like scissors), and you'll only need one extra hand to get it up. They run anywhere from forty to one hundred dollars, so watch for a sale.

10. Remember that dew accumulates at night as well as in the morning, whenever there's a drastic shift in temperature. This will affect any and all paper you have out, including books. We have the books we sell covered in plastic, except for the one on display (it's going to get flipped through a thousand times anyway). Large baggies will suffice if you don't have a shrink-wrapper. Also, any display cards and whatnot that you want to use again should be covered in plastic or on a display card/tray.

11. Always have free stuff to give away, be it stickers or a bowl of candy-shelled chocolates. Whatever swag you choose to offer, make sure it has your logo on it. You're welcoming people to your "home" to shop, so be as hospitable as possible. I saw one lady having a tea party right there, selling her homemade brews, giving people a chance to chat while they browsed. What an awesome idea.

12. Sell a variety of stuff, and be creative with your display. If you only have the same type of item, you'll quickly lose the buyer's interest. Also, if what you have is on the pricey side, count on many less sales. One woman was selling gorgeous hand-made tomes for BoS (Book of Shadows) use, but they were *waaaay* too expensive, starting at $50. She went home without selling a single item, because no one could afford what she was offering.

13. Wheel n' deal, but not until the last day. We primarily sell CDs, usually for ten dollars a piece. On the last day, we're likely to flip to "three for twenty" deals, buy two, get one free, that sort of thing. Just be sure you're not drastically cutting into your profit, and don't severely undercut other merchants - they're not your enemies.

14. Get a credit card machine of some sort - you'll get more sales. We use an old-school swiper (scroll down for my comments on that link), because many places out in the boonies won't pick up a signal, even with our phone. Just remember to turn in those slips promptly, so the buyer won't forget about that purchase and call the credit card company. Receipt books, sold at most office supply stores, help a great deal.

There are now devices which turns your smart phone into an instant, electronic credit card swiper. They even allow customers to sign for their purchases, and it emails them a receipt. Welcome to the future, as they say.

Now true, it'll only work if there's a cell phone signal, so keeping the oldschool swiper on standby is a good idea. Be sure to find out ahead of time if where you'll be vending gets decent bars.

15. Think ahead of time about what is standard fare at merch booths. You can count on everyone selling candles and incense, so come up with something you always wished was available but hardly ever see. When you bust out the uniques, count on selling more.

16. If you're selling clothes of some sort, think critically for a second. Perhaps you're a svelte twenty-something, but not everyone is. With shirts, the biggest seller size-wise is XL we've found, so stock up on that size. Also, be sure to have a couple XXL and XXXLs on hand as well (in the most popular styles, of course), as Pagans, like everyone else, come in all shapes and sizes. Also, think of unisex products, like beautiful wraps and jewelry.

17. On that tangent, think what items a CAMPER needs, like stakes, natural sunblock and hygiene products - that sort of thing. Also, consider selling ice-cold, bottled water if it's really hot. (Just so you know, $8 a bottle is NOT a fair price.) And, every festival has potential for rain, so selling Pagan-y umbrellas and ponchos ain't such a bad idea. On that note, every festival has a potential to get REALLY cold at night, so having long-sleeve shirts, hoodies, skull caps and such, even in July, is a good idea. Just be sure the fest isn't already selling these types of items.

18. Leave out a sign-in sheet for customers to receive emails from you, so they will hopefully visit your website and shop with you year-round. (You *do* have one, right?) We're creative by having a contest for a prize pack, consisting of a little bit of everything we have to offer. People love getting free stuff and entering contests even more. Just be polite and don't spam the hell out of the people who signed up.

19. Be prepared for people who just love to argue about anything, and will stir up shit if you disagree with them. Sometimes, I swear it just makes those jokers feel good to always be right. Be as neutral and as polite as possible, even if your customer is a drunken bastard who really needs to take a chill pill. Just smile and nod, and they'll eventually go away. Remember what mom always said about not saying anything? She really was right.

If you *really* wanted to make an effort, find one thing on their person you truly do like and say so. It will deflect their angst into a topic they're happy to go into detail about, and you just might win them over on a sale. (It's happened to me a number of times.) Also, NEVER talk shit about someone at the festival, because it WILL get back to them eventually.

20. Supply shopping bags, and offer them freely to overburdened shoppers. Ahead of time, pack a business card, brochure or post card in each one so the recipients will hopefully visit your online store in the future. Also, offer storage space if you can swing it, as not everyone is there for the duration. We've gotten quite a few stock-up sales for taking these two steps – just for helping people out and being friendly.

If you hold peoples' stuff, put their bags behind the counter near your valuables, staple the bags shut and write their names on the bags. Be sure to disclose you will do your best, but you are not responsible for loss or damage.

Do You Still Want to Vend?

I've already listed the basic vending rules, but because there are a lot of variables involved, I figure I should elaborate further on the subject. If you've ever considered doing this, please read further. It's a lot of fun, but there is also a lot of work involved.

After you have decided where you'll be going, you need to plan your inventory around what your future customers will want or need. Standbys like herbs, incense, t-shirts, books and Pagan-themed crafts are pretty easy to stock up on, since there are Pagan wholesale shops that carry all these things. However, if you've never been to a fest before, you will be in for a rude awakening when you arrive and discover ten other booths are selling the exact same things. Therefore, while it will make your outdoor shop appear credible, it will not really stand out, unless you undercut everyone else (and become the Undacuttin Mutha Fukka in the process).

I highly suggest you do not vend the very first time you attend a fest, even if you get the notion you can recover at least a portion of your trip costs this way. For one thing, there is <u>never</u> a guarantee in sales when it comes to being a retailer. Never. The Big Box stores everyone loves to hate actually operate at a loss for several years at each one of their locations. They need to figure out what the locals buy the most and which hours to operate. If *they're* losing money, you should have no expectation of a high profit margin.

My uncle was a famous and rather successful pizza maker here in Chicago, as well as the owner of a popular night club. From his decades of experience, the single most important piece of advice he ever gave me was,

> *"If you break even your first year, you're extremely lucky. If you keep your head above water for two years, you're successful. And if you make it a decade, you're probably certifiably insane."*

Hmmm... yes. I've had people refer to us as being kinda nuts; I'll get back to you in a few more years whether or not we're wearing straight jackets.

Keep in mind while yes, my uncle's operating costs must have been scary to even think about, he was selling something people buy regularly. He also got to know his regulars' favorites over several months and years, where to cut corners cost-wise (while still maintaining quality.) and experienced quite a bit of trying and failing. The new kid on the strip just doesn't have this.

If you've been to at least a handful of various fests, then you should have an inkling of what you would really like to sell. Think critically: What was the one or two things you wish someone had, and what would you consider to be fair prices for them? Hang out on eBay and see what people are asking for these things. Some people low-ball, some people are deceptive upon final sale by jacking up shipping costs, and some people are Teh Stoopids. Compare *those* prices to what other online retailers are asking, and that should give you a fair price margin.

Keep in mind too, whatever it is you want to sell, you are going to need to get it. Many wholesalers offer full return policies, though you will have to closely follow their rules and pay the return shipping yourself. Others may have ten to fifteen percent restocking fees. And others still make all their sales final. This is *in addition* to having to cover the shipping costs back to the wholesaler. Read the fine print.

Also too, if you're new at this, steer clear of back-ordering. What this means is if an item you requested is not in stock at the time, they'll ship it to you at a later time and charge you only for what was shipped (usually). However, when the item comes in, they will not necessarily honor any discounts you previously earned at the time you placed the order, and they may even charge you separate shipping. Again, read the fine print.

If you are looking to sell truly unique items, see if you can make what you sell. That can be books, altar tools, crafts, CDs, clothing, toys, home goods, musical instruments... anything you wish you could buy as a customer. Yes, making your own products may significantly cut costs, but doing so requires time and (raw) materials.

If you want to sell handmade jewelry, you will need to have enough to fill the average folding table, which runs six to eight feet long and two feet wide. Of course, that's the sort of thing you would want to spread out, but that's still a lot to make. Go into your jewelry box and spread out everything you own as if you were to sell it. Unless you're the Queen of England, you probably do not have nearly enough to attract customers. People will walk by your nearly-empty table thinking you're not yet set up. Most of these types of vendors spend at least a few hours a week just making jewelry, many at least an hour a day, with each piece taking at least an hour. Do the math.

And too, what you make needs to be of a quality equal to what customers are used to seeing for the price you're asking. If you want to sell your music on a CD, the only way to ensure people will justify paying $10 for it is if you offer them a CD that looks like what they would expect to find at any record store. While we artsy folks like to think our works should stand on their own merits, the average person does not. Sad but true.

After you've amassed a quantity of merchandise, set up your booth at home. Clear out your living room if you have to. Play with your booth until it looks like a fest shop you think will have storefront appeal. Is it plain? Is it crowded? Will people get the *Ooh! Shiny!* vibe? Have a couple friends stop by and get their opinions.

Dressing up your booth is just as important as the stuff you're selling, because it too adds value to your merchandise. If your store looks like a flea market booth, people will believe what you're selling is not worth much. Trust me on this. However you dress up your booth is going to need to be lugged down, set up, endure all kinds of outdoor weather, torn down, lugged back home and then stored away. Phew. Just thinking about all that work is tiring.

Tarps and vending tents are your friends. Bins are your friends, too. Make sure what you use is easily collapsible yet sturdy and will be able to withstand a downpour. Every fest I've attended has had some type of moisture involved. Not once was the weather completely ideal even when it was, because once the sun went down and rose again, condensation reared its ugly head.

If you're selling books or other paper products, shrink-wrap or bag them, even if they're used. (Mark them as new or used.) Also, have a place to lock up your good stuff, even if it's your car. (Many fests allow vendors to park next to their booths, but they may be charged extra. Take advantage of this.) This is again where I encourage a lot of planning.

Before you pack up your inventory, clearly price each and every item. If you're selling a lot of the same thing, but perhaps in different sizes, styles and colors, you can post several price sheets around your area. Make them pretty, straight-forward and easy to read. However, do not be surprised when you get every other customer asking how much this is, if you have that in another size, or even if there is another booth selling the same thing for less - even if you hang a neon sign. People can <u>and will</u> ask what you determine to be the stupidest questions. Be prepared to be patient.

One other thing that will help draw people to your booth is having a schedule sheet prominently posted. A hundred times each day, someone is going to ask when the multi-faith workshop is happening. If you have it posted in front of your table, people will see it and may look at your wares immediately in front of it. But, if you place it behind you, though still in a very conspicuous area, they'll lean forward to read it while you get in that precious first impression.

I've also detailed about accepting payment, but I wanted to elaborate on another topic besides cash, check or charge: Trading and bartering. Some fests let you do that, and some don't. Know ahead of time if this is acceptable, and if it is, and you want to, I personally wouldn't advertise it. Rather, let the customers ask you. By posting a sign that says,

"*Yes! We take trades!!*", you are discouraging people from paying you, and outside the fest, no one else is going to accept your trade - not the kid at the gas station, not the waitress and not your wholesaler. It is what it is.

And finally, I've already said this, but I'll say it again: Be patient, be polite and be ready to talk to your customers. Bring a friend to relieve you, don't read a book or jabber jaw too much while you're on duty, and make sure you're comfortable. An empty booth invites shoplifting, inattentiveness has people walking away, and crabby vendors all but ensure customers will not consider buying from you now or anytime in the near future. When people stop by, drop whatever it is you're doing and say hello with a smile. Yes, it's probably hot, and you might be sitting in a bowl of ball soup, but that doesn't mean you have to let your customers know you're uncomfortable. Hand and box fans (if possible), plenty of shade and water, food, empty bladders and comfy chairs will make you a much more pleasant vendor.

If you are *still* interested in vending, and I hope you are, start your inventory planning now while it's the dead of winter. A little here and a little there will not only give you something to do and look forward to, but it will chase the winter blues away.

A Guide to Pagan Camping

When the Fest is Over

"There is a time for departure even when there's no certain place to go."
— Tennessee Williams

Has it been a week already? Where did the time go? Yup, it's time to pack it up and head back into the "real world" of dirty streets, water and air, and unhappy, money- and power-hungry people. Wow, that's enough to make anyone depressed. I know of many people who have seriously considered moving out to the "boonies" after their first primitive camping experience just for that reason alone. Even so, it's time to shake it all out and pack it all up.

I like to focus on the positive when a vacation is over. While I'm packing up and getting ready to leave, I think about all the fun I had while I was there and things I learned as well. Since I'm an urban Pagan in the truest sense of the word, having to leave the countryside and new friends I've made can be especially hard, but a relief just the same. After all, even the most comfortable air mattress can't replace my big warm bed at home, and no stuffed animal can replace my fur baby.

A good idea is to ensure everyone gets in one last good meal before getting started, especially if you have a grueling drive ahead of you. While you eat, you can discuss who will be doing which tear-down duties. I would suggest preparing something that's light, easy, creates few dishes and gives you extra energy. You don't want your group to need a nap before they help pack up.

The other option is, if everyone is hung over and just wants to get going, is to say to Hell with it and find a restaurant to chill at after you leave. I suggest a sit-down joint that has a buffet, where you and your Covenmates can hang out at for a while, nurse some coffee and not argue over the menu. Since Ron's omni and I'm veg, we often choose truck stops, since many of them have a lot of everything, and their buffets are only around five dollars per person.

Pack everything into your car the same way you did to get there. Remember to keep the little cooler in the car so you have something to drink and munch on for the trip back home. One thing that's nice about going home is you always bring back less than you brought in (unless you went crazy at the merchants' booths). Therefore, you should have a much easier time packing. Remember to use your whisk broom and dustpan to sweep out the inside of your tent before you pack it up; you don't want to be folding up any twigs that can puncture the tent, or trap any unwary insects.

Even if you think you're done, you're not. Always, always, always take an extra look around for something you left. Pick up ALL of your garbage and any that someone else left as well. Sprinkle a little grass seed over your site to help the ground recover from your visit. Check that your fire pit is completely out and not smoldering. I personally dump a full gallon of water into my pit until the coals are floating. The remaining ice melt in your cooler serves this purpose well.

If you hadn't gotten a chance to really look around the grounds, now's the time. Get in that hike you've been meaning to do and say good-bye to the land that welcomed you. Exchange email addresses and phone numbers with others you've met. Stop by the merchants tearing down and see if they're willing to still sell anything. Many times, you'll get a <u>huge</u> discount on items just so the merchant has less to pack.

Remember to sign out from the grounds if it is required. If you haven't fulfilled your work shift duties, please offer to do so now. While monetary compensation is the traditional form of owing up to your neglect, what these festivals really need is labor. It takes *people* to make them work, not money. So please don't forget to do your share, preferably before the last minute.

Finally, as you wind down the road back from whence you came, you'll be bringing back more than just your gear. You'll be bringing back fond memories for many years to come.

Part II

My Fool-Proof Pre-/Camping Recipes

> *"If more of us valued food and cheer and song above hoarded gold, it would be a merrier world."*
> –J.R.R. Tolkien

The following pages feature many recipes right out of my own kitchen, both indoor and outdoor. Some recipes, like the artisan bread, I recommend you make at home to wrap up and bring with you, and some I suggest you do the prep work before you leave.

I hope you and yours enjoy them as much as me and mine. To me, cooking is my spellwork, with my kitchen serving as my altar and everything in it as my tools. (Gourmet grocery stores and farmers' markets are my temples.) Everything I do in there is with love, and it's the one place I feel truly at ease.

Enjoy!

Sample Festival Menu

> *"Right after I got here, I ordered some spaghetti with marinara sauce and I got egg noodles and ketchup."*
>
> –Henry Hill, *Goodfellas*

No one really wants standard camp food; they've just grown accustomed to accepting that's just how ya do. Not me, and you probably don't, either. So, let's have some fun with a menu and use some of my recipes to put it all together. (If I didn't list a recipe, you can easily find one on the Internet – this is just an idea to get you started.)

This sample menu revolves around the Pagan Spirit Gathering's schedule, as it's one of the longest *and* longest-running fests. Obviously, you can adjust this to cut days out of this menu as needed or change the menu day for the Potluck Feast at the fest you're attending. I attempted to plan each meal to be healthy, delicious and as easy as possible, with recipes to follow. I also erred on the side of caution by providing too much information rather than not enough.

Kindly be aware too, I have considered you may have very limited (if any) grocery store access, having to bring everything in with you before entering, perishable foods expiring and vegetarians wishing to dine with you. And yes, I know full well folks tend to draw weary of cooking extravagant meals after a few days. Even we gourmet foodie types need a reprieve after baking in the sun and/or getting soaked on outdoors over several days, but that doesn't mean we eat bland, generic crapola. And PLEASE remember to drink lots of fluids; water is best.

Meal Beverage Choices: for any day, mix/match/select

Breakfast: (Decaf) Coffee/(Herbal) Tea/(Frozen Concentrated) Juice/(Soy/Rice/Nut) Milk/Water
Lunch: Iced (Decaf) Coffee/(Herbal) Sun Tea/Lemonade/Soda/Water
Dinner and Dessert: (Decaf) Coffee/Tea/(Herbal) Sun Tea/(Hard) Lemonade/Beer/Wine/Soda/Water

---

Day of Arrival: Sunday

Breakfast: --- (Road Food)
Lunch: Cold Cut Sandwiches and Relish Tray (very easy) (Finger foods while setting up camp)
Dinner: Pre-Packed Hearty Foil Stew (very easy) (Will be tired from journey and setting up)
Dessert: Peach Cobbler (easy) (Need a quasi-healthy sugar rush for late night drumming and dancing!)

Potluck Feast Day: Monday

Breakfast: Granola, Yogurt and Sliced Fresh Fruit (very easy) (Will be tired from night before and need energy after long night of partying!)
Lunch: Cold Cut Sandwiches and Relish Tray (very easy) (Will want to consume most time to getting to know people and preparing for Potluck Feast)

Dinner: *Potluck Feast*
Dessert: *Potluck Feast*

Third Day: Tuesday

Breakfast: Pancakes, Scrambled Eggs and Canned Hash (easy) (Need to consume eggs!)
Lunch: (Vegetarian) Grilled Burgers/Brats/Sausages/Hot Dogs (with veggies and condiments), Chips, Canned Baked Beans
Dinner: Grilled Steaks/Portabella Caps with Onions, Foiled Baked Potatoes and Pre-foiled, Frozen Corn on the Cob Halfs (Hard-frozen steaks will be thawed by then and needed to be cooked!)
Dessert: Baked Apples (very easy)

Midnight Madness Day: Wednesday

Breakfast: Crossaints with Butter and Jam, Sliced Fruit (very easy) (Heavy dinners should be followed by light breakfasts!)
Lunch: Cheese and Cracker Platter, Sliced Fruit (very easy) (Need to use up any lingering berries, consecutive hot days make people tired and not want to exert much energy)
Dinner: Spaghetti with Pre-Made Red Sauce, Bruschetta and Salad (easy) (Vendors will want something quick and easy to make that doesn't require a watched, roaring fire! Also, artisan breads will need to be consumed by this time.)
Dessert: Pre-made Italian Cookie Assortment (very easy) (Hopefully the cookies haven't already been eaten!)

Fifth Day: Thursday

Breakfast: Eggless Breakfast Burritos (easy)
Lunch: Soft Tacos (easy) (Refried beans from breakfast, uses up last of tomatoes, lettuce and cheese)
Dinner: Chili and Corn Bread Bake (easy) (Start after lunch, ready by dinner)
Dessert: Fried Bananas (easy) (They'll be getting brown by this point!)

Sixth Day Friday

Breakfast: Pancakes and Pre-Cooked Bacon (easy)
Lunch: Pre-Packaged Heat and Serve Meals (very easy) (At this point, some become so lethargic they eat straight from the can!)
Dinner: California Casserole (easy) (Uses up now completely thawed frozen vegetables)
Dessert: Instant Vanilla Pudding (very easy)

Final Full Day: Saturday

Breakfast: Hot/Cold Cereal (very easy) (Let group make their own meal!)
Lunch: Pre-Packaged Heat and Serve Meals (very easy) (Meh. Too tired, hot and cranky to cook anymore! Want to sleep, shop and attend workshops instead!)
Dinner: Red Beans and Rice, Corn Bread (easy) (Start after lunch. Make one final, good but easy dinner. Go out with a bang!)
Dessert: Pre-Made Bread Pudding (very easy)

Departure Day: Sunday

Breakfast: Hot/Cold Cereal (very easy) (Quick and easy meal, easy clean-up for packing up.)
Lunch: --- (Road Food)
Dinner: --- (Road Food)
Dessert: --- (Road Food)

Fool-Proof Artisan Bread

This pretty, hearty white bread recipe is intended for preparing at home and bringing along for the ride. It has a wonderful crust and is the perfect base for sandwiches. Sliced thick and toasted, it's even better for bruschetta, Panini sandwiches or garlic bread.

You will need:

- Large, clean work surface
- Stand mixer capable of kneading dough (optional)
- 2 large mixing bowls
- 1 cookie sheet
- 1 mixing spoon
- 1 Measuring cup and spoons
- Nonstick cooking spray
- Aluminum foil
- Bread knife
- Basting brush
- Cooling rack
- Zippered plastic bag (optional)
- Clean hands, apron and hair tie (recommended)

Ingredients:

- 5½ cups all-purpose flour (1½ cups retained and separated)
- 2 cups lukewarm water (about 100°F) (¼ cup separated)
- ¼ cup olive oil
- 3 tablespoons butter, softened (1 tablespoon reserved)
- 1 teaspoon sugar
- 1 teaspoon salt
- ½ teaspoon active dry yeast

Total time: 5 hours, 45 minutes
Serves: 12-16

Step 1:

Tie back hair, put on apron and wash hands thoroughly. In a mixing bowl, pour ¼ cup water and sugar, stir until completely dissolved. Add yeast and set aside for 5-10 minutes, until yeast has bubbled and foamed. Reserve remaining yeast packet in plastic bag and refrigerate. (If yeast has not proofed, try another package.)

Step 2:

After yeast has been proofed, pour in remaining water. Blend 4 cups of flour (with dried measuring cup) and salt well in second bowl, then slowly stir in with water. Mix with spoon until it becomes a sticky paste. Remove spoon, add butter and 1 additional cup of flour. If a stand mixer is not available, grease hands with olive oil and begin kneading dough over bowl, stretching and pulling for about 15-20 minutes. Add remaining ½ cup flour as needed during this process. When dough becomes translucent when stretched, cover bowl with aluminum foil, coated with nonstick cooking spray, and set in warmest area available. Allow to sit approximately 3 hours or until dough has at least doubled in size.

Step 3:

When dough has risen, grease hands, remove dough and knead in a punching and folding fashion to remove pockets of air bubbles, about 5 to 10 minutes. Coat cookie sheet and second bowl with nonstick spray, place dough on sheet, form into (somewhat flattened) ball and cover with bowl. Transfer dough back to warm area for ½ hour to 1½ hours for second rise until doubling again.

Step 4:

Before removing dough, preheat oven to 400°F. Remove bowl, reform ball, slit dough four times (spaced evenly), then gently coat with olive oil. Transfer to oven and bake 25-30 minutes, rotating once halfway through. When bread appears to have finished baking, remove from oven, turn over and flick with thumb and middle finger (thump). Listen for hollowness. If yes, transfer to cooling rack for 15 minutes to finish the baking process. Slather slits with softened butter. Slice into ½" to 1" servings as needed. Store bread in an airtight container (can be stored without refrigeration 2-3 days).

Beer Bread

If you have never been good at making bread, this recipe I developed will fool everyone into thinking you're a bakery God/dess and is Lugh approved! No kneading, no exerting hours of energy required, and boy howdy does it taste delicious. Beer bread pairs well with melted butter, spiced fruit jams or various stews (chili).

You will need:
- Large, footed, well seasoned Dutch oven
- Hot coals on campfire
- Stirring spoon
- Measuring cup, spoons
- Bottle opener
- Basting brush
- Large mixing bowl
- Cutting board
- Bread knife
- Aluminum foil
- Pot holders
- Apron

Ingredients:
- 1-9 ounce bottle quality wheat beer (weiss), room temperature
- 3 cups all purpose flour
- ½ cup butter, softened
- ¼ cup apple juice
- ¼ - ½ cup sugar (depending on sweetness preferred)
- 1 tablespoon baking powder
- 1 teaspoon salt
- Olive oil (as needed)

Total time: 1-1/2 hours
Serves: 12-16

Step 1:

Warm Dutch oven directly over coals and don apron. In bowl, mix together dry ingredients. Add juice, then slowly add beer and continue to mix. "Roll the bottle" to get last of yeast. Dough will be very foamy at first, then form into an extremely sticky batter. Cover in greased foil and let rise 30 minutes in sunny location.

Step 2:

Using potholders, remove Dutch oven from coals and grease entire interior with oil, including lid. Grease spoon and spoon in dough into Dutch oven. Cover and place directly on coals, with 6 on top, for about an hour. Shift coals periodically to avoid hot spots.

Step 3:

During last 10 minutes of baking, brush on oil. When finished baking, the top will be very crusty and golden brown, yet the insides will be soft. Remove from heat, uncover and allow to sit at least 10 minutes before transferring to cutting board. Allow to cool another 10 minutes before slicing, wrapping unused portion in airtight container. Can be stored up to 3 days.

Stove Top Jam

If you find yourself with a bunch of well-ripened fruit, be it at camp or at home, please don't toss it. Instead, turn it into delicious jam everyone will enjoy. It's great on crackers and bread or as a topping for pancakes, French toast or just about any dessert.

You might want to wear an apron for this, as the bubbling back splash can get a bit messy. Permanently stained clothes are unpleasant.

You will need:
- Small sauce pan
- Stirring spoon
- Measuring cup, spoons
- Small jar with tight-sealing lid
- Potato masher
- Kitchen utility knife
- Cutting board
- Citrus juicer and zester
- Apron
- Vegetable peeler (optional)

Ingredients:
- 2 cups ripe fruit
- 1 cup sugar (optional)
- 1 tablespoon water
- 1 orange or lemon, juice, pulp and juice
- 1 teaspoon candied ginger, minced (optional)

Total time: 1 hour
Serves: (varies)

Step 1:

Put on apron. On a cutting board, cut down fruit to 1/4" cubes, composting rotted pieces. Remove skin if necessary. (Note:

apples and grapes contain pectin which will help thicken jam.) Toss into sauce pan with water, orange and ginger and mash over medium heat. When well mashed, use spoon and stir constantly until near desired consistency, preferably until sticking to spoon a bit.

Step 2:

Remove from heat and allow to cool in pan. When cooled to room temperature, spoon into jar and close. Will last about one week refrigerated.

Super Chunky Red Sauce

My guys love this, and so will you. I've cultivated this recipe over several years, honing in just the right amount of flavor to hearty texture. This is definitely a sauce that sticks to even the thickest of pastas - even lasagna noodles. Things can get rather messy, so be sure to keep a sponge or towel handy, because sauce sticks.

Do not use your Dutch oven for this, as it's too acidic, resulting in a metallic taste. Mobster types (how *you* doin'?) should be cautious not to drop their guns in the pot for the same reasons. (Fugetaboutit!) Also, the milk can be omitted to make it vegan, though it really does help cut the acidity of the tomatoes as well as bring out their sweetness. (I unfortunately do not feel soy/rice/nut milks are good substitutions in this particular case, as they don't serve the purpose.)

You will need:
- Large stew pot
- Long stirring spoon
- Ladle
- Utility kitchen knife
- Cutting board
- Measuring cup/spoons
- Can opener
- Apron and hair tie
- Clean hands

Ingredients:
- 3 - 28 ounces cans stewed tomatoes, whole
- 2 - 6 ounce cans tomato paste
- 1 large onion, sliced
- 1 large green pepper, chopped
- 3 large carrots, peeled and sliced
- 3 stalks celery, chopped

- 1 large zucchini, sliced
- ¼ cup milk
- ¼ cup sugar
- 1 tablespoon parsley, dried
- 1 tablespoon basil, dried
- 1 tablespoon oregano, dried
- 1 teaspoon garlic powder
- 1 teaspoon pepper
- 1 teaspoon salt (add more to taste)
- ½ teaspoon red pepper flakes

Total time: 4-6 hours
Serves: 8-12

Step 1:

Don apron, tie back hair and wash hands thoroughly. Empty tomatoes into pot and mash well with hands for at least 5 minutes. Add remaining ingredients and stir until well crushed and blended.

Step 2:

Over medium heat, bring to simmer. Cover and reduce heat to medium low. Stir sauce at least every half hour, scraping from bottom to top in order to prevent tomatoes burning and scorching.

Step 3:

When sauce is nearing desired thickness, remove lid and raise heat to medium. Stir frequently, watching for scorching and burning. Remove from heat and allow to slightly cool before serving and/or canning.

Lori's Grilling Sauce

This is probably my most beloved of sauces, and I believe in sharing it rather than keeping it all to myself. Even skeptical, critical folks, raised on true barbecue and who swear by their own family secrets, have not-so-secretly confided in this city-slicking Yankee something serious is going on. Of course, I'm quick to point out it's not entirely all about the sauce; my marinade, rubbing and grilling methods are part of a team that play equally on the field.

So whether you're using it on the grill or for dipping fried potatoes, feel free to whip some up and see for yourself if my claims hold water. It's also the same base I use for baked beans; I just cook it with prepared Navy beans and bacon (or a porky-type flavoring).

You will need:
- Stew pot
- Stirring spoon
- Measuring cup/spoons
- Kitchen utility knife
- Cutting board
- Can opener
- Serving vessel
- Apron and hair tie

Ingredients:
- 3 - 28 ounce cans stewed tomatoes, pureed
- 1 - 4 ounce can tomato paste
- ½ cup apple cider vinegar
- ½ cup brown sugar, packed
- ¼ cup honey
- 1 small onion, minced
- 1 tablespoon liquid smoke
- 1 tablespoon Worcestershire sauce
- 1 teaspoon garlic powder
- 1 teaspoon pepper

- 1 teaspoon salt (to taste)
- 1 teaspoon Dijon mustard
- 1 teaspoon cilantro, dried
- 1 teaspoon basil, dried
- 1 teaspoon oregano, dried
- ½ teaspoon cayenne pepper

Total time: Approximately 2 hours
Serves: (varies)

Step 1:

Don apron and tie back hair. Add all ingredients in pot over medium heat, stirring well. Bring to simmer and reduce heat to medium-low. Stir occasionally, scraping from bottom to top.

Step 2:

When sauce reaches desired thickness, remove from heat and allow to cool. Pour into bowl (if grilling), canning jars or serving vessel.

Marinade Recipe and Method

It is my opinion whatever it is you're throwing on the grill over the fire should have some sort of seasoning, be it salt and pepper, barbecue sauce or yes, a marinade. While fire makes everything taste good, there is no doubt in my mind this can be improved upon. Meats and vegetables alike take well to this concoction, and there is at least one Worcestershire sauce out there that is vegan. (Most of them have anchovies as an ingredient, of which I'm not a fan.)

You will need:
- Large mixing bowl
- Large (1 quart) freezer bags
- Whisk
- Aluminum foil
- Measuring cup/spoons

- Utility kitchen knife
- Cutting board
- Meat tenderizer and plate (optional)

Ingredients:
- 4 cups water
- ¼ cup Worcestershire sauce
- ¼ cup steak sauce
- ¼ cup olive oil
- ¼ cup balsamic, apple cider or red wine vinegar
- 1 small onion, diced
- 1 clove garlic, pressed
- 1 tablespoon salt
- 1 tablespoon pepper
- 1 tablespoon dried parsley
- 1 tablespoon thyme
- 1 tablespoon paprika
- 1 tablespoon oregano
- 1 tablespoon rosemary
- 1 tablespoon basil

Total time: 1 hour
Serves: (varies)

Step 1:

If applicable, pound meat with tenderizer, or chop vegetables into 1" cubes and set aside. Add ingredients to bowl and whisk vigorously until it begins to foam. Add item(s) to be marinated to mixture and cover with foil. Refrigerate at least one hour.

Step 2:

Transfer item(s) to freezer bag and, over sink, pour in some of marinade. Squeeze out as much air as possible and seal. Insert into second bag, again squeezing out air, and sealing.

Note:

If item is meat, lay flat in freezer until frozen solid. When packing in cooler, be sure to store at very bottom. Cook after thawing. If item is a vegetable or especially potato, it should be cooked promptly. Some vegetables do not tolerate freezing and thawing well and will therefore rot.

Bruschetta

Have you ever wanted to offer an appetizer that is quick and easy but has people assuming it took a lot of effort? Then look no further. This recipe is not only easy and requires few ingredients, but the main one makes great use of artisan bread that is teetering on the stale side.

While the birds may appreciate the tastiness, it's you and your guests who should be enjoying such labors right to the very last crumb.

You will need:
- Cast iron skillet
- Potholders
- Small mixing bowl
- Basting brush
- Utility kitchen knife
- Cutting board
- Measuring cup/spoons

Ingredients:
- 4 slices artisan bread, 1" thick each, lightly toasted on one side
- 4 plum tomatoes, sliced
- ¼ cup chopped fresh basil
- 2 tablespoons shredded Parmesan cheese
- 1 clove garlic, minced
- 2 teaspoons balsamic vinegar
- 1 teaspoon olive oil
- Sea/Kosher salt and course ground black pepper to taste

Total time: 10 minutes
Serves: 4

Step 1:

Arrange bread on skillet, toasted side up. Stir vinegar, oil and garlic gently with brush in bowl. Evenly distribute mixture by brushing on each bread slice. Top with tomatoes, basil then cheese.

Step 2:

Toast bread for only a few moments. Sprinkle with salt and pepper. Serve immediately.

Breakfasts

"All happiness depends on a leisurely breakfast."
—John Gunther

Skillets

One of the easiest, yet tastiest, things to do is make a skillet breakfast. What's even better is you can do everything but actually cook it ahead of time. Before you leave, crack and scramble some eggs with a little milk in a bowl, enough to feed yourself and your other campers, or use extra firm tofu. Add some hash browns and your favorite ingredients: diced vegetables, meat, shredded cheese (or veg versions) and seasonings. Fold everything over well and then pour everything into a well-made freezer bag (I like to double the bags).

You can also portion them out by using multiple sandwich-size freezer bags. You'll want to squeeze out as much air as possible, both for freshness and to save that precious space in your cooler. A smart idea is to freeze the mixture before putting it in your cooler. Not only will your breakfast survive the trip without spoiling, but you'll be helping your cooler stay cold. Remember to grease your griddle well, as eggs, most sautéed vegetables and cheese love to stick to the griddle.

Pancakes

I have yet to meet a person who doesn't like pancakes. Pancakes are easy, fun and have that warm, comforting aroma to them. Again, you can prepare the mixture ahead of time and simply pour the batter onto a hot griddle. Adding blueberries is an added treat. You can even make an apple or strawberry compote to serve on top, instead of maple syrup.

However, if you plan on serving any sides, such as eggs or meats, be sure you plan ahead of what to cook first. No one likes cold eggs, so make them last. Bacon, sausage, hash, ham and steaks, on the other hand, should be made first; just cover and set that aside. Of course, vegan versions are almost always available, some of which taste remarkably/eerily similar to the porky stuff.

Cereals

Hot and cold cereals are the standards, whether at home or abroad. It's simple, easy and nourishing; perfect for the early riser. Since milk doesn't travel well, buy it right before you get there, stored in your large cooler. You may also consider trying boxed soy milk, since it needs no refrigeration until after it's been opened, though you may want to chill it overnight.

Hot cereals require a little more work, but with so many "instant" varieties on the market in small pouches, all you'll need is a little hot water from your kettle.

Other Ideas

Sliced fruit, with some yogurt and granola makes for a light, refreshing and beautifully presented meal. The best part is you don't have to start up the fire, especially if you had a late night, or you really want to get packing and head back home. You may also want to try adding or replacing your meal with toast, English muffins or bagels, topped with butter, cream cheese, honey, peanut butter and/or jam. Be creative and go with what you enjoy at home.

A comfort food my mom used to prepare my brothers was some peanut butter, sliced bananas and honey, sandwiched between warm slices of raisin toast. (Remember vegan versions of all of these things are readily available at most supermarkets.)

Orangy Muffins

Here's a neat little trick for baking muffins over the coals while adding an extra bit of flavor. Dad told me about this method years ago, and yes indeedy, it works well and is absolutely delicious. The best part is, it makes great use of the rinds you would otherwise compost when making freshly-squeezed orange juice.

You will need:
- Hot coals
- Mixing bowl
- Aluminum foil
- Stirring spoon
- Kitchen utility knife
- Cutting board
- Tongs
- Dining spoons

Ingredients:
- 8 medium oranges, halved and pulp reserved
- Prepared muffin batter (try blueberry)

Total time: Approximately 20 minutes
Serves: 4-8

Step 1:

Mix batter per package instructions. Using spoon, carefully fill each orange rind 2/3 full with prepared muffin batter. Tear one square sheet of foil and loosely wrap from bottom to top, shaping bottom into a flat surface. Using tongs, place on hot coals and bake approximately 10-15 minutes, or until muffins become golden brown.

Step 2:

Using tongs, remove from coals and set on heat-resistant surface. Carefully peel back foil on top and allow to cool 10 minutes. Serve.

Breakfast Pudding

Are you tired of lumpy oatmeal when what you really want is a quick, healthy bowl of delicious? Then whip this up and treat your group to something that's more like dessert than breakfast. This recipe is perfect for using leftover rice from the night before.

You will need:
- Sauce pan
- Stirring spoon
- Measuring cup/spoons
- Can opener
- Soup service for 4

Ingredients:
- 2 cups prepared brown rice
- 2 cups mixed berries
- 1 - 14 ounce can sweetened condensed milk
- ½ teaspoon cinnamon
- ½ teaspoon vanilla extract
- ½ teaspoon nutmeg

Total time: 5 minutes
Serves: 4

Step 1:

Mix ingredients in pan. Stir constantly over medium heat until it reaches a boil. Remove from heat, stir well and serve.

Easy French Toast

Here's an quick, beautiful breakfast you can whip up for your group that really tastes that much better outdoors in a cast iron skillet. It's a great way to use up bread that's going stale, eggs that need to get used and those still glowing embers you don't feel right about extinguishing.

You will need:
- Cast iron skillet or griddle
- Glowing embers or full-on campfire with grill
- Potholder
- Spatula
- Whisk
- Mixing bowl
- Measuring cup/spoons
- Kitchen utility knife
- Cutting board
- Service for four

Ingredients:
- 16 - 1" thick slices of bread, day old (try multi-grain).
- 8 eggs
- ¼ cup milk
- 1 tablespoon vanilla extract
- Nonstick cooking spray or butter
- Powdered sugar, cinnamon and sliced fruit to garnish
- Maple syrup, jam or fruit compote, butter, whipped cream (optional)

Total time: 15 minutes
Serves: 4

Step 1:

Place skillet directly over coals or on grill over flames and allow to warm. While doing so, crack eggs and whisk vigorously. Add milk and vanilla, again whisking vigorously until thick and foamy.

Step 2:

Check pan for warmth. Droplets of water should "dance" but not evaporate (too hot). Lift pan with potholder and coat bottom with spray or butter. Dip bread into foamy mixture for a couple seconds on each side, gently pinching off excess. Toss on skillet, without cramming, about 5 minutes on each side, until golden brown.

Step 3:

Using spatula and potholder, cut bread diagonally in skillet and place triangles onto plates, 8 pieces each. Dust with powdered sugar and cinnamon and garnish with sliced fruit. Serve warm.

Lunches

"Ask not what you can do for your country. Ask what's for lunch."

—Orson Welles

Sandwiches

Show the world the kids at the franchise submarine joints aren't the only creative sandwich makers out there. Since most of the prep work can be done at home, all you'll need to do is set everything out nicely and watch as your hungry campers help themselves. Offer fancy sandwich rolls, thinly sliced deli meats and cheese (veg options always available), Romaine lettuce leaves, sliced veggies, sprouts and fast food condiment packets. Be sure to have your wash basins out so everyone can wash their hands before they handle the food.

Relish Trays

In addition to, or in place of sandwiches, offer a healthy feast in itself of nothing but finger foods. Think Thanksgiving afternoon and you'll know where I'm going. At home, prepare a freezer bag full of carrot and celery sticks and another of broccoli and cauliflower florets. Offer a jar of pickle spears and black olives, a bag of your favorite snack chips or crackers and sliced meat and cheese; don't forget the dip. You can also add some fresh fruit, such as apples, bananas, oranges and grapes in a large bowl for a nice presentation, perhaps garnished with berries.

Remember to pack a small portion of this for the car ride to and from your camp site for a fresh and healthy alternative to truck stop junk food.

Here's a vegan and delicious veggie dip recipe that's Omni-approved and easy. Just dice up a bunch of green onions and mix it in a container of veggie sour cream and add a touch of powdered garlic. It works every time.

Salads and Sides

Sure, anyone can make a garden salad, even Wendy's, but even this rabbit food muncher gets tired of the same ole, same ole. Why not try to take it up a notch?

A quick salad I actually just made for myself requires no more than a tomato, a cucumber, some salt, pepper, garlic powder and balsamic dressing. Go easy on the seasonings and dressing if you're a novice. Vinegar has a way of overdoing a good thing.

Cut it up into cubes and toss it all together. To make it pretty while adding flavor, chop up some cilantro and onion. A single lime can be used too: half juiced and half cut in semi-circles for flair.

Pasta salad isn't all that hard, either. Try using rotini pasta with sliced black olives, tiny broccoli florets, slivered carrots, Italian dressing and Parmesan cheese (or nutritional yeast if you like).

Potato salad is fairly easy, too. Just cube and boil some potatoes until tender (*not* mushy) and cool. Add in some (vegan) mayo and a good squeeze of mustard if you like, along with some diced onion, celery and carrot. Bring out the flavor with salt and pepper.

Soups and Stews

Do away with the can. Nothing says comfort like homemade soup, and there are so many varieties to choose from. The easiest, most fun soup to make is vegetable. Remember the story of Stone Soup and go with whatever you find in the refrigerator. Simply chop and add your favorite veggies, herbs and seasonings to some boiling water and let it simmer until everything is tender. Add rice or barley to both thicken and add texture; add cubed meat for the omnivores.

Making a soup a stew merely requires adding some flour or corn starch to the soup; be sure to stir well. Even making it portable is simple; either use your trusty freezer bags, doubled over, or use a cleaned spaghetti jar or two. Bring along some crackers or bread; part of what makes soup comforting is sopping it all up.

Other Ideas

Fire up those logs and go Americana. Nothing beats a good barbecue in summer, and even your vegan friends can attest to that, provided you make a couple small changes to suit their dietary requirements. Whether you go for burgers, hot dogs, steaks, barbecued chicken, ribs, or skewered veggies, anything cooked over an open fire tastes better. Add some side dishes like potato salad and cole slaw, roasted corn, baked beans and sliced watermelon to really make you feel good inside. Don't forget the condiments, even in packet form.

Remember to portion out your meat ahead of time and, by using your new best friend, the freezer bags, have it marinate while you travel. The ancient Mongolians kept their meat tender while they traveled, so why can't you?

Happy Snacky Cracker Platter

Here's an extremely easy yet very pretty appetizer dish you'll have a hard time making, because you'll be tempted to eat every other one. My advice is to go ahead and nosh a few of the imperfect ones, so as long as you don't deliberately goof them up.

You will need:
- Large serving platter
- Kitchen utility knife
- Cutting board
- Butter knife
- Can opener
- Basting brush
- Small mixing bowl
- Clean hands

Ingredients:
- Variety of 1 inch toasted bread and/or crackers
- 4 ounces Swiss cheese, sliced thin and to fit crackers
- 4 ounces sharp cheddar cheese, sliced thin and to fit crackers
- 4 slices (veggie) luncheon roast beef, sliced slightly smaller than cheese
- 4 slices (veggie) luncheon roast turkey, sliced slightly smaller than cheese
- 1 - 4 ounce can sliced black olives, drained
- 1 - 4 ounce can sliced water chestnuts, drained
- 1 small red bell pepper, slivered
- ¼ cup Italian vinaigrette

Total time: 10-15 minutes
Serves: (varies)

Step 1:

Arrange bread and crackers on tray from the center outward in a circular pattern. Be sure the crackers alternate in variety.

Step 2:

Pick up and brush each cracker with a touch of dressing, then return to tray. Apply Swiss and roast beef to half of crackers, cheese first, other half with cheddar and turkey. Add one layer of water chestnuts, cross each cracker with red pepper, then top with one olive slice. Serve.

Veggie Wraps

This is, quite possibly, my favorite summer lunch. And once you try it, it may very well be yours as well. Some may simply refer to it a merely a salad in a tortilla, but I would rather it be called pure bliss.

You will need:
- Large work surface
- Mixing bowl
- Whisk
- Table spoon
- Measuring cup/spoons
- Vegetable peeler
- Kitchen utility knife
- Cutting board
- Clean hands

Ingredients:
- 4 extra large tortillas (burrito size)
- 1 Romaine lettuce heart, shredded
- 2 plum tomatoes, sliced
- ½ cucumber, peeled and sliced
- 1 avocado, sliced
- 1 small onion, sliced paper thin
- 1 small green pepper, sliced thin
- 1 - 8 ounce tub spicy hummus
- 1 - 4 ounce package alfalfa sprouts
- ¼ cup cranberries, dried
- ¼ sunflower seeds, salted
- ¼ cup mushrooms, sliced
- ¼ cup balsamic vinegar
- 1 teaspoon basil, dried
- ½ teaspoon Dijon mustard
- ½ teaspoon pepper

Total time: 5 minutes

Serves: 4

Step 1:

In bowl, combine vinegar, mustard and seasonings. Whisk ingredients together well until a slight foam surfaces. Set aside.

Step 2:

With clean hands, scoop a heaping spoonful of hummus onto each tortilla in the bottom center and spread upwards, divided until all hummus is used. Distribute remaining ingredients, fluffing and adding sprouts last, then lightly drizzle with whisked dressing.

Step 3:

Carefully fold tortilla inwards, beginning with the bottom then tucking in each side, then wrap tightly. Hummus will act as a glue. Turn over, slice in half and serve.

Lettuce Wraps

Are you intolerant to gluten? Did you run out of bread? Do you just want something quick, crisp and cool on a hot summer's day? Then try making these mini wraps for a surprising twist on an old favorite. Your guests will squeal with delight after tasting it.

You will need:
- Mixing bowl
- Table spoon
- Whisk
- Kitchen utility knife
- Cutting board
- Can opener
- Vegetable peeler
- Service for 4

Ingredients:
- 1 - 15 ounce can chickpeas, chilled and drained
- 2 plum tomatoes, chopped
- 1 small onion, diced
- 1 large carrot, peeled and slivered
- ½ cucumber, peeled and chopped
- 12 red lettuce leaves
- ¼ cup balsamic vinegar
- 1 teaspoon basil, dried
- ½ teaspoon Dijon mustard
- ½ teaspoon pepper
- ½ teaspoon salt

Total time: 5 minutes
Serves: 4

Step 1:

Whisk vinegar and spices in bowl. Add and toss remaining ingredients. On cutting board, scoop heaping spoonful into lower center of each lettuce leaf and wrap tightly. Cut wraps in half and serve.

Tuna Pasta Salad

On a hot summer's day, there is nothing quite like a chilled pasta salad to cool you down. It's quick, light, healthy and has just the right amount of contrast to stave off lunchtime boredom. Be sure to make the pasta at breakfast so it's ready to go by lunch.

If you don't care for tuna, it can be omitted, though it does add a good amount of flavor and protein. Chickpeas are a decent substitute. Also, while not mentioned, the salad mixture can be chilled after preparing for an hour to help meld flavors, though you may be too tired, hot or hungry to work or wait

You will need:
- Medium pot or pan
- Mixing bowl
- Large serving spoon
- Measuring cup/spoons
- Kitchen utility knife
- Cutting board
- Can opener
- Service for 4

Ingredients:
- 4 cups rotini pasta, chilled
- 1 - 4 ounce container albacore tuna or chickpeas, chilled and flaked (and drained if needed)
- 2 plum tomatoes, chopped
- 1 small onion, diced
- 1 small red bell pepper, diced
- ½ cup broccoli florets, chopped
- 1 - 4 ounce can sliced black olives, chilled and drained
- ¼ cup Italian vinaigrette
- 1 tablespoon Parmesan cheese
- 4 lettuce leaves

Total time: 5 minutes

Serves: 4

Step 1:

Mix together ingredients, except lettuce, in bowl. Set aside.

Step 2:

On each plate, lay one leaf of lettuce, curl side up. Divide salad equally on top of each leaf. Serve.

Dinners

"Make your having dinner out become The Event of the Night, instead of just the beginning."
–John Waters

Pastas

Can you boil water, boys and girls? I knew you could. Now how about adding a little pasta in there? Good. Now, why not have a little fun with that and round off your meal. At home, grill and cube some chicken or Italian sausage, onions and peppers, then add a jar of your favorite pasta sauce. Bag it up, freeze it and bring it with you to camp. Add this to freshly cooked and drained pasta while it's still piping hot and give it a real good stir.

Depending on how cold the mix is and how hot you like your food, a little extra heating may be required. Don't forget the topping. Pasta and red sauce always goes good with the Parmesan cheese, and vegans out there know the great alternatives available.

Ethnic

So many ethnic dishes can be prepared with little to no thought. After all, it's almost always all about the sauce. Many items can be prepared vegetarian and vegan, and still sticks to your ribs as darn good eatin'. boxed vegetarian taco filling is so good, even our son will eat it. It's soooo much less work than frying up hamburger, draining the grease (and finding a place for it), then adding the seasoning. Just add water and a little oil.

Home Away from Home

When I make dinner at home, I think of three things: what meat, what veggie and what starch. Since I make dinner straight after I get home from work, I also focus on how much time it's going to take, and how many pots I'm going to need. If you go this method, you're guaranteed to make a good and easy meal. Try these combinations, prep everything except the starch and add the remainder, and stir it all together: shells and cheese, prepared with frozen California blend veggies and cubed chicken breasts; egg noodles, prepared with cream of mushroom soup, tuna and frozen peas; cubed and roasted beef brisket and gravy with garden vegetables, boiled garlic potatoes; thin strips of stir-fried pork with soy sauce, frozen stir fry vegetables, rice or ramen noodles.

Meat and Potatoes

One of the simplest meals to make, yet costs a small fortune at any decent restaurant, is a good steak. Portion out a good sized, good quality cut of beef for each person and rub it hard in your favorite seasonings; I prefer powdered garlic, black pepper, seasoned salt, and a touch of steak sauce. Then take out your frustrations on it and pound it even harder with a kitchen mallet. Then, bag it in your favorite marinate and bring it on down. Wrap some baking potatoes in aluminum foil and, using a fork, poke a few holes into them on every side. Throw them along the sides of the fire (not directly in), and give them an hour or until soft.

If you feel the need to actually eat a vegetable, may I suggest roasting some corn? You'll need to boil them, in husk, for an hour before roasting them over the fire. I like to add seasoned salt and butter to the water to get extra flavor into the corn. I make skewered veggies right alongside the NY strips and baby back ribs for my friends, using the same seasonings. YUM! Also, an experiment that worked well on corn is this, with no butter or salt needed:

Buy the frozen mini corn cobs and wrap them in aluminum foil. Place them by the potatoes and cook for the same length of time. The smoky flavor seeps into the corn and cooks it just right. It came out sweet, tender and flavorful. My fellow campers had their doubts, thinking it would turn into corn flakes, but nope. Damned good eatin'.

Other Ideas

Give Cooky and his chuck wagon a run for their money. Nothing tastes better than having meats and veggies repeatedly basted and slowly rotated over an open fire, letting all of that smoky flavor reach into every crack and crevice. Sure it takes time to work a spit, but if you're willing, go for it. Shish kabobs are not only fun to eat, but they're easy and quite healthy, too. Serve them over some flavored rice and you have a perfect meal. Scratching your head about a side vegetable? Have a pre-made salad, with lots of fresh veggies, and some homemade dressing. Want an idea for a centerpiece? Give my beautiful watermelon display a try. Everyone loves them at potlucks.

Sausages and Kraut

One of Dad's favorite dishes indoors or out, this hearty one-pot entree is sure to be yours as well. Whether you choose to use your campfire or propane stove, this recipe is about as easy as one could ever want. And yes, veggie sausages are most definitely available.

You will need:
- Large Dutch oven
- Slotted serving spoon
- Kitchen utility knife
- Cutting board
- Measuring cup
- Vegetable peeler

Ingredients:
- 4 cups water
- 2 pounds small red potatoes, cleaned and quartered
- 2 pounds carrots, peeled and chopped
- 3 stalks celery, chopped
- 1 large onion, chopped
- 2 crisp apples, cored, peeled and chopped
- 2 pounds favorite smoked sausage, sliced into 1" portions
- 2 - 14 ounce cans sauerkraut

Total time: Approximately 1 hour
Serves: 8

Step 1:

Warm Dutch oven over heat, add water and bring to boil. Add all ingredients, except kraut, in order listed. Reduce heat, cover and simmer until potatoes and carrots are tender and onion is translucent.

Step 2:

Add kraut, cover and simmer 10 minutes longer. Serve.

Lori's Curry

Is it hot? It could be. Is it filling? Most definitely. Is it authentic? Not really. This aromatic stew is a little somethin'-somethin' I whip up when the hankering hits me, and I don't feel like killing myself looking for parking on Devon Avenue. Try it, and I guarantee you'll like it, topped over basmati rice or paired with naan bread for dipping.

You will need:
- Large stew pot
- 2 large mixing bowls
- Large aluminum roasting pan
- Aluminum foil
- Skillet
- Stirring spoon
- Kitchen utility knife
- Vegetable peeler
- Can opener

Ingredients:
- 1 - 16 ounce bag dried lentils, prepared (about 7 - 8 ounce cans)
- 2 cups red potatoes, diced
- 2 cups tomatoes, diced
- 2 cups carrots, peeled and sliced
- 1 head cauliflower, cut into florets
- 1 cup onion, diced
- 1 cup water
- 1 cup milk
- ¼ cup olive oil
- ¼ cup garam masala
- 1 teaspoon cumin seeds
- 2 teaspoons garlic powder
- Chili paste, cayenne pepper powder or "rooster sauce" to taste and if desired
- Salt and pepper to taste

Total time: Approximately 30 minutes (not counting lentils)
Serves: 25

Step 1:

Bring water to boil in pot. Add potatoes and carrots, boil 10 minutes. Add cauliflower, continue to boil five minutes longer. Drain, add with lentils to roasting pan, cover and set aside.

Step 2:

While pot is still hot, add olive oil and onions. Sauté until caramelized. Add spices, water and tomatoes and stir until simmering. Add milk and heat until hot, stirring constantly. Combine into roasting pan and blend together. Taste for heat, flavor and saltiness; add as desired. Serve warm.

Stuffed Cabbages (Galumpkis)

Growing up, I looked forward to Mom making these for us, and she usually made them when we were "between checks", if you catch my drift. With or without meat, these little bundles of deliciousness will fill your group up and fuel them with plenty of energy to spare.

You will need:
- Stock pot or large Dutch oven
- Large aluminum roasting pan
- Large mixing bowl
- Skillet
- Sauce pan
- Aluminum foil
- Serving spoon
- Stirring spoon
- Kitchen utility knife
- Can opener (optional)
- Tongs

Ingredients:
- 3 quarts boiling water
- 2 cups cooked brown rice
- 2 cups browned ground pork, drained or prepared TVP
- 1 head cabbage, bottom sliced off and leaves peeled separately
- 2 - 26.5 ounce cans or bags spaghetti sauce, any variety
- ½ cup milk
- Salt to taste

Total time: 1 hour
Serves: Approximately 25

Step 1:

Bring water to boil, salted preferred. While doing so, cook rice, brown ground pork and gently separate leaves from cabbage.

Gently add leaves one at a time with tongs. Boil until tender. Wash pan.

Step 2:

Mix ground beef and rice in bowl, along with 1-1/2 cans of sauce. Taste and add salt as needed. Cover with aluminum foil and set aside.

Step 3:

Just before leaves are tender, retrieve washed sauce pan and add milk and retained sauce. Occasionally stir over medium heat until hot.

Step 4:

When cabbage leaves are tender, gently retrieve them from pot and place them in roasting pan, curl side up. Spoon one tablespoon full of pork and rice mixture into each leaf, then folding like a burrito, fold side down. Continue until a full layer is made, then pour half milk and sauce mixture over. Make second layer the same way. Spoon remaining pork and rice mixture along edges. Cover with aluminum foil, serve hot.

Easy Camp Chili

This hearty chili recipe is so easy and delicious; there is simply no way you *can't* make it for your group. Meat can be whatever type you prefer (many like venison or buffalo to beef) or go with a vegan option. Top it with brown rice or oyster crackers and your favorite shredded cheese, and pair it with either corn or beer bread.

You will need:
- Dutch oven
- Can opener
- Stirring spoon
- Measuring cup/spoons
- Kitchen utility knife
- Cutting board
- Ladle
- Soup service for 4

Ingredients:

- 1 pound lean ground meat (or prepared TVP)
- 1 - 16 ounce can red kidney beans, rinsed
- 2 - 16 ounce cans pinto beans, rinsed
- 2 - 16 ounce cans stewed tomatoes
- 1 large green pepper, diced
- 1 large yellow onion, chopped
- 2 stalks celery, diced
- 1 bunch green onions, diced and separated
- 3 cloves garlic, pressed
- ¼ cup chili powder
- ¼ cup paprika
- 1 teaspoon brown sugar
- 1 teaspoon cumin seeds
- 1 teaspoon cayenne pepper
- 1 teaspoon cilantro, dried
- 1 teaspoon oregano
- 1 teaspoon thyme

- 1 teaspoon parsley, dried
- 1 teaspoon salt
- 1 teaspoon pepper
- 1 tablespoon olive oil (optional)

Total time: Approximately 1 hour
Serves: 4-6

Step 1:

In Dutch oven, brown meat (add olive oil if very lean or using TVP) with all seasonings and onion, green pepper, garlic, celery and cumin seeds until meat is browned and onion has caramelized.

Step 2:

Stir in tomatoes and simmer 10 minutes uncovered, stirring occasionally. Add beans, stir and simmer 10 minutes longer. Serve warm.

Shepherd's Pie

And just how pray tell can this be made while camping without an oven? Easy - read the recipe and find out. It's so hearty and easy, you'll wonder why you haven't tried creating this before.

You will need:
- Dutch oven
- Skillet
- Two large mixing bowls
- Serving spoon
- Stirring spoon
- Potato masher
- Vegetable peeler
- Kitchen utility knife

Ingredients:
- 2 cups browned ground beef, drained or prepared TVP
- 2 cups mashed potatoes
- 2 - 8 ounce cans brown gravy (beef or mushroom flavor)
- 1 bag frozen peas, steamed
- 1 cup peeled and diced carrots, steamed
- 1 cup canned fried onions
- Salt and pepper to taste

Total time: 1 hour
Serves: 12

Step 1:

Prepare mashed potatoes, set aside in mixing bowl and wash pan used. Fry beef and steam peas and carrots. In second mixing bowl, combine gravy, beef and vegetables. Taste and season to liking.

Step 2:

Press mashed potatoes in Dutch oven along bottom and sides. Pour in stew mixture. Top with mashed potatoes, topping that with onions. Cover and bake until hot. Serve warm.

Camp Stir Fry

I like to think of a stir fry as more than just a way to clear out the crisper drawer and getting rid of leftover meats. Whipping up such an entree is an easy, quick, delicious and extremely filling way to satisfy even the most ravenous of camping guests.
Serve over brown or white rice, or any variety of Asian noodles.

You will need:
- Large wok or skillet
- Small sauce pan
- Whisk
- Stirring spoon
- Kitchen utility knife
- Cutting board
- Measuring cup/spoons
- Can opener
- Service for 4

Sauce ingredients:
- 1 - 12 ounce can stewed tomatoes
- 1 tablespoon orange marmalade
- 1 tablespoon peanut butter (chunky style preferred)
- 1 tablespoon soy sauce
- 1 tablespoon honey
- 1 teaspoon powdered ginger
- 1 teaspoon garlic powder
- 1 teaspoon red pepper flakes

Ingredients: (Choose 4 to 6)
- 1 cup raw meat, prepared shrimp or extra firm tofu, cut into 1/2 inch cubes
- 1 bunch green onion, diced, greens reserved as garnish
- 1 large onion, chopped
- 1 large green pepper, chopped
- 1 bunch broccoli florets
- 3 stalks celery, chopped
- 3 large carrots, peeled and slivered

- 1 cup bok choy, chopped
- 1 cup napa cabbage, chopped
- 1 - 8 ounce can water chestnuts
- 1 - 12 ounce bag bean sprouts (garnish only)
- 1 - 8 ounce can bamboo shoots
- 1 cup pea pods
- 1 cup mushrooms, sliced
- + 1 tablespoon peanut or sesame oil

Total time: 30 minutes
Serves: 4

Step 1:

Whisk all sauce ingredients over medium heat until well blended. Cover and simmer, gently whisking occasionally to prevent burning.

Step 2:

Warm wok with oil over medium heat. Add onions, celery and carrots first for 5 minutes. Raise heat to high, then meat until browned. Add remaining ingredients, lightly tossing occasionally until vegetables are still crisp yet slightly tender. Add sauce.

Step 3:

Transfer stir fry onto plates over rice or noodles. Serve.

Desserts

"Vegetables are a must on a diet. I suggest carrot cake, zucchini bread and pumpkin pie."
—Jim Davis

I can't believe I never really touched on this topic before, but I guess I can atone for my actions now.

I know a lot of folks think having a dessert while camping is nothing more than the S'mores standby. And hey, I love me my s'mores as much as the next guy. But there are a few things you can easily prepare even without an oven or a fridge that will really surprise everyone.

- On the lighter side, mix a can of pumpkin (*not* pumpkin pie mix) with a large container of vanilla (soy) yogurt for pumpkin pudding. (You can add a little brown sugar if you like to sweeten it up) Sprinkle some cinnamon (or better yet, nutmeg) on top.

- Of course, baked apples can be done with aluminum foil and placed right outside the coals. All you need to do is core some firm apples (Fujis are good for this), and fill them with cinnamon sugar (one part cinnamon, three parts sugar). Wrap then in foil and let the salamanders do their job until soft.

Canned Cakes

So you'd like to serve cake while camping, but you have no interest in attempting to bake one away from your home oven. No problem; you can do that ahead of time, and these little cakes will be moist and delicious even on the last night. I've adjusted this time-tested method a bit and yes indeedy, the cakes slide right out, they're cute as a button and taste like they're fresh out of the oven.

Folks have been shipping these "cakes in a jar" for decades to our troops all over the world, especially to commemorate birthdays. The troops love these little slices of home so much, it's become all but a requirement for special care packages, or even not so special.

Caution: When you bring these to the fest, people will come out of the woodwork to beg for a bite, which will turn into your portion.

You will need:
- 5 sterilized 16 ounce wide-mouth canning jars and lids
- Potholders
- Cookie sheet
- Mixing bowl/spoons
- Narrow stirring spoon
- Packaging material to avoid breakage
- Canning sterilizing equipment (boiling pan, tongs)
- Bread or cake knife
- Dessert service for ten

Ingredients:
- 1 package favorite chocolate cake mix and ingredients required
- 1 container favorite frosting
- Nonstick cooking spray

Total time: 45 minutes

Serves: 10

Step 1:

Preheat oven to 350°F and sterilize jars (standard boil method). Follow cake batter instructions. Spray interior of jars well. Evenly distribute batter with spoon into jars without touching sides, filling to no more than half of each. Place jars with mix on cookie sheet on center rack of oven. Bake until center comes out clean with toothpick.

Step 2:

While baking, sterilize lids in water. Immediately cover with hot lids after removing cakes from oven and screw on rings. Set aside to cool.

Step 3:

Wrap jars with frosting and perhaps birthday candles, in packaging materials such as shredded paper, in smallest cardboard box available. Be sure there is no shifting whatsoever and jars are not touching. When packing with gear, pack within clothes or bed rolls as an extra precaution against shifting, cracking and breakage.

Step 4:

When serving, slide each cake out onto a plate and cut in half. Place sliced part down on service plate and add frosting. Distribute to group. Will last up to 1 year in jar.

Super Easy Trifle

Whether or not you know how to make angel food or pound cake, you can certainly whip this dessert up for your group. It's pretty, decadent and a step above most campers' potluck contributions. You're guaranteed to get lots of praise for both its presentation and taste.

You will need:
- Large serving bowl, clear trifle dish if possible
- Large mixing bowl
- Serving spoon
- Whisk
- 3 table spoons
- Can opener
- Clean hands

Ingredients:
- 4 boxes instant vanilla pudding (and required milk)
- 2 pound cakes
- 1 can pie filling
- 1 tub whipped topping or cream

Total time: 10 minutes
Serves: 25

Step 1:

In a mixing bowl, whisk pudding and milk required per box instructions. Set aside to continue thickening. Open can of pie filling. (Blueberry and cherry are popular choices, though I still prefer apple.)

Step 2:

In the serving bowl, add a few dollops of pie filling to form bottom layer. Break off some pieces of cake to form second layer. Using a different spoon, add a layer of pudding. Using a third spoon, dollop in whipped cream for fourth layer, then follow with another layer of cake. Continue until all/most ingredients are used. Serve.

Crispy Rice Treats

With this recipe, even your youngest campers can make this time-tested dessert or afternoon snack. And thanks to vegan marshmallows being on the market, the entire festival can enjoy them worry-free. Shoot for popular brands for extra (enriched) vitamins and minerals.

You will need:
- Dutch oven or stew pot
- 1 stirring spoon
- Rectangular baking pan
- Aluminum foil
- Clean hands

Ingredients:
- 4 - 5 cups crispy rice cereal
- 1 - 16 ounce bag marshmallows
- ½ cup butter
- 1 teaspoon vanilla extract

Total time: 2 hours, 15 minutes
Serves: 12

Step 1:

Melt the butter in Dutch oven or stew pot, stirring in vanilla. Stir in marshmallows, a few at a time. After all marshmallows are melted, remove from heat and slowly stir in the cereal one cup at a time.

Step 2:

Wash hands. Transfer the mix into pan and press very firmly until there's very little "give". Allow to cool an hour, press firmly again, then cut into squares. Allow to cool another hour before serving. Cover with aluminum foil (can be stored 2-3 days without refrigeration).

Potlucks

"I went to this restaurant last night that was set up like a big buffet in the shape of an Ouija board. You'd think about what kind of food you want, and the table would move across the floor to it."
—Steven Wright

There are a *gazillion* recipes out there for potluck contributions, but too few of them specifically cater to ones that can be whipped up out in the outdoor kitchen.

What's worse, the bulk of the ones I've come across are either too small of a contribution (there should be 25 servings for a fest contribution) or they're the standard pasta or salad dish. I say, stray from the ordinary and come up with something you'd be proud to serve the Goddess.

Here are the rules:

- It should be in a large casserole dish, bowl, roasting pan or pot and accompanied with a serving utensil (think catering service size so everyone is sure to get some).
- If it's an entrée, you can go with just a protein or in combination with a starch and/or vegetable.
- You should already enjoy it yourself.
- Avoid making something like a salad or a pasta dish, because it seems everyone brings that.
- A list of ingredients should be included. One better, provide photocopies of the recipe used to share with others.

- If meat/dairy and/or eggs are ingredients, please be sure those items were kept consistently cold before using.

Holiday-Inspired Dressing

The argument is this: Stuffing goes in the bird, dressing is prepared separately. With that being said, this is *dressing* that is not just for Thanksgiving anymore. It can indeed be paired with turkey, but it's also great with chicken, pork or as the main entree. And because this recipe is vegan, everyone can indulge in this healthy, guilt-free bite of Americana – even if it's not wrapped around a holiday.

You will need:
- Hot coals
- Large aluminum roasting pan
- Aluminum foil
- Large sauce pan
- Large serving spoon
- Measuring cup/spoons
- Utility kitchen knife
- Cutting board
- Vegetable peeler
- Can opener
- Clean hands

Ingredients:
- 1 - 1 pound bag herb seasoned stuffing mix
- 1 - 12 ounce can pumpkin
- 1 large onion, diced
- 1 whole stalk celery, diced
- 2 large carrots, diced and peeled
- 3 small apples, diced, cored and peeled
- 1 can vegetable broth
- 1 - 1 pound tube vegan breakfast sausage
- ½ cup raisins
- ½ cup cranberries, dried
- 1 tablespoon pomegranate juice
- 1 tablespoon lavender flowers, dried
- 1 tablespoon thyme
- 1 tablespoon ground sage

- 1 tablespoon rosemary

Total time: 1 hour
Serves: 25

Step 1:

Wash hands thoroughly. In roasting pan, mix bread crumbs, corn meal, pumpkin, broth, sausage and seasonings with hands and set aside.

Step 2:

In sauce pan, combine remaining ingredients, apples first, and cover tightly. Sweat over medium heat for about 20 minutes, shaking pan every so often to deter burning or scorching. Empty contents into roasting pan, including the accumulated water. Again mix with hands until it reaches a loafy consistency.

Step 3:

Cover pan with aluminum foil and place on grill over coals for at least 30 minutes or until crust forms along sides. Check periodically for hot and cool spots and adjust accordingly. Serve warm.

Loaded Deviled Eggs

I never cared for the standard recipe, especially in comparison to Mom's version that I played with a bit. Yes, a main ingredient is processed junk food, laden with MSG. But around here, no feasting holiday would be without my eggs. Besides, our son absolutely *insisted* I include this in the book. Our friend John commented they're like little breakfast appetizers (eggs, cheese, tortillas, bacon).

As a bonus, the eggs can be hard boiled at home and stored in the cooler for easy transport. Just be sure to mark the carton so the wrong eggs aren't accidentally cracked open during a morning rush.

You will need:
- Serving tray
- Large mixing bowl
- Aluminum foil
- Table spoon
- Measuring cup/spoons
- Kitchen utility knife
- Cutting board
- Clean hands

Ingredients:
- 1 dozen hard boiled eggs
- 1 - 2 ounce bag of nacho cheese flavored tortilla chips, crushed well
- ½ cup (imitation) bacon bits
- ½ cup mayonnaise
- 1 tablespoon Dijon mustard
- 1 teaspoon paprika
- 1 teaspoon turmeric

Total time: 1-1/2 hours
Serves: 24

Step 1:

Wash hands thoroughly. Carefully shell eggs and toss shells in compost heap if acceptable. Gently slice eggs lengthwise and remove yolks. Place whites on serving tray and yolks in mixing bowl. Place tray in cooler. (Will help chill tray and keep eggs fresh.)

Step 2:

Mix all but paprika in bowl, mashing yolks well. Retrieve hollowed eggs and fill with mixture. Cover with foil and place in cooler 1 hour.

Step 3:

Retrieve deviled eggs from cooler right before serving. Remove foil, sprinkle with paprika and serve.

Watermelon Centerpiece

Have you ever wanted to contribute something to a potluck that was easy, beautiful, delicious *and* healthy? If you can carve a pumpkin, you can definitely do this fun, flavorful and healthy dish.

You will need:
- Large aluminum roasting pan
- Large mixing bowl
- Large slotted serving spoon
- Chef or bread knife (must be long and sharp)
- Cutting board
- Apron
- Marker
- Melon baller
- Clean hands

Ingredients:
- 1 large watermelon
- 1 cantaloupe, seeded
- 1 honeydew melon, seeded
- 2 cups berries (strawberries, blueberries, raspberries, etc.)
- Crushed ice (as needed)

Total time: 30 minutes
Serves: 25

Step 1:

Put on apron and wash hands well. Locate the center of watermelon. Outline cut marks to transform into wide basket, handle 2" wide. Cut out the two portions outlined and set aside. Carefully empty remaining melon using a melon baller. Place balled melon in bowl and set aside. Cut a hole into bottom of basket to serve as drainage. Further design basket if desired and place into pan.

Step 2:

Retrieve two portions of watermelon, slice them directly down the middle into four quarter slabs. Slice each quarter slab now needs into wedges, about 1" thick. (Remaining pieces can be salvaged for more melon balls.) Set wedges aside for later decorational use.

Step 3:

Use melon baller on cantaloupe and honedew and toss into bowl with crushed ice. Mix melon balls with berries and arrange them in basket. Line up the watermelon wedges around the basket. Serve.

Note:

Juice from watermelon can be used with jigger of vodka and crushed ice for a cool mixed drink.

Southwest Burritos

Oh yeah, you want this, and so does everyone else. Whether you use the filling in burrito-sized tortillas as an entree or rolled in small corn tortillas as appetizers, you can guarantee everyone is going to be asking for the recipe. Feel free to hand out some photocopies.

You will need:
- 5 quart pot
- Fork
- Measuring spoon
- Utility kitchen knife
- Cutting board
- Can opener

Ingredients:
- 1 cup white rice
- 4 cups water
- 2 - 15 ounce cans black beans, drained and rinsed
- 1 - 12 ounce can white or yellow kernel corn, drained
- ¼ cup cheddar cheese, shredded
- 1 - 4 ounce tub sour cream
- 2 plum tomatoes, diced
- 1 large onion, diced
- 1 fresh jalapeno pepper, diced (seeds and membrane removed)
- 1 lime, juiced
- 2 teaspoons dried cilantro
- 2 teaspoons garlic powder
- 2 teaspoons chili powder
- 2 teaspoons black pepper
- 2 teaspoons salt
- 2 teaspoons olive oil
- ½ teaspoon cayenne pepper

Total time: 30 minutes

Serves: (varies)

Step 1:

In pot, bring water to boil over medium heat with juice, half of oil, jalapeno and seasonings. Add rice, stir and cover. Lower heat to simmering and cook 20 minutes until tender and fluff rice.

Step 2:

Add beans, veggies and remaining oil, raise heat back to medium and stir until warm. Fill in tortillas with cheese and sour cream and roll accordingly.

Spicy Guacamole

As I was making this for dinner, it dawned on me how other people may wish to also make some as a fresh dip, taco topping or burrito filling. And yes, it is indeed filling, with healthy fats to boot.

You will need:
- Serving bowl
- Serving spoon
- Measuring spoon
- Utility kitchen knife
- Cutting board

Ingredients:
- 2 ripe avocados
- 1 lime, juiced
- 1 small onion, chopped
- 1 plum tomato, chopped
- 1 fresh jalapeno pepper, diced (seeds and membrane removed)
- 1 teaspoon dried cilantro
- 1 teaspoon garlic powder
- 1 teaspoon chili powder
- 1 teaspoon black pepper
- 1 teaspoon salt
- ¼ teaspoon cayenne pepper

Total time: 10 minutes
Serves: (varies)

Step 1:

Squeeze juice into bowl and stir in spices. Cut open avocados, remove rind and pits. Dig out meat and mash well in bowl. Add onion, tomato and jalapeno. Fold in well and serve.

Cucumber Salad

This is probably the easiest recipe I have to offer, and yet it's incredibly delicious. I just could not fail to include it, especially when it's matched with some serious Tex-Mex tastiness.

You will need:
- Serving bowl
- Slotted serving spoon
- Measuring spoon
- Utility kitchen knife
- Cutting board
- Vegetable peeler

Ingredients:
- 1 cucumber
- 1 lime
- 1 teaspoon dried cilantro
- ½ teaspoon salt

Total time: 5 minutes
Serves: 4

Step 1:

Slice lime in half, deeply score and squeeze out juice into bowl. Compost remainder. Sprinkle on salt and cilantro and stir. Peel cucumber, slice in half lengthwise and chop into semicircles. Mix cucumber into bowl, spooning over as much juice as possible. Serve.

Fee Phi Faux Pho

This is a take on the noodly goodness that is Pho (pronounced "fuh"), the Vietnamese beef soup the Gods bestowed upon us mere mortals. While making the soup itself is rather tedious, time-consuming and requires a lot of exotic spices, I made a quick noodle dish of this on the cheap and served it at a recent Witches' Ball. The pans were completely devoured, and I made A. Lot. In order to switch this over to primitive camping mode and not go broke in the process, as well as to keep the veg*ns happy, here's what...

You will need:
- Large aluminum roasting pan
- 5 quart Dutch oven or pot
- Serving spoon
- Stirring spoon
- Two coffee filters, cheesecloth, etc.
- Kitchen utility knife
- Vegetable peeler
- Small, tight-sealing jar
- Approximately 6 inches food-grade twine

Ingredients:
- 12 packages ramen noodles (beef or Oriental flavor)
- Approximately 1 quart water
- 4-6 jalapeno peppers, sliced
- 3 medium carrots, slivered
- 3 plum tomatoes, halved and sliced
- 2 limes, halved and sliced
- 1 - 12 ounce bag bean sprouts
- 1 bunch chopped green onions, greens separated
- ½ cup lime or lemon juice
- 6 whole cloves
- 3 whole star anise, broken
- 2 tablespoons soy sauce
- 1 tablespoon olive oil
- 1 cinnamon stick

- 1 teaspoon dried mint leaves
- 1 teaspoon fennel seed
- 1 teaspoon dried cilantro
- 1 teaspoon dried parsley
- 1 teaspoon powdered coriander
- 1 teaspoon dried basil
- 1 teaspoon powdered ginger
- 1 teaspoon garlic powder
- 1 teaspoon chili powder
- 1 teaspoon black pepper
- 1 teaspoon chili paste (more to taste)
- 1 teaspoon cumin seed

Note: Some of these spices are pricey or hard to find, so feel free to "do without". (I purposely excluded a ½ teaspoon of ground cardamom for this reason.) Fresh is best in my opinion, so if you are able, by all means go for it. Just remember to double the amount of fresh herbs to dried. (Fresh ginger and minced garlic should be added to warmed olive oil until sautéed, then add cumin seeds at very end of process.)

Total time: Approximately 30-45 minutes.
Serves: 25

Step 1:

At home, wrap cinnamon stick, star anise, fennel seeds and cloves in a couple coffee filters, being careful not to puncture them. Combine cilantro, parsley, coriander, basil, ginger, mint, garlic powder, chili powder, juice, black pepper, soy sauce and chili paste in jar.

Step 2:

At camp, heat olive oil until reaching smoke point in a Dutch oven or large stew pot. Sauté green onion bulbs until caramelized. Add cumin seeds until they begin to pop; this will happen quickly. Then, toss in the pouch, jar of spices as well as half the ramen noodle packets and carrots. Add water to half full and bring to a boil. Add and cook noodles until tender; there should be very little liquid left. Add tomatoes a few minutes prior to noodles reaching tenderness. Taste for saltiness and add more seasoning packets if preferred. (Save remaining seasoning packets for another recipe.)

Step 3:

Remove the spice pouch, pour everything into a large roasting pan, then garnish with lime, jalapenos, sprouts and retained greens. Serve warm.

Red Beans and Rice

If ever there was a one-pot meal that defines Creole cooking, this is it. What's even better is this recipe is so quick and easy, anyone can make it. It's not quite authentic, but it's really close. If a veggie version of the sausage is used, everyone will be happy to join you for dinner, especially if you side it with some hot and tasty corn bread.

You will need:
- Stock pot
- Long stirring spoon
- Long serving spoon
- Can opener
- Potato masher
- Kitchen utility knife

Ingredients:
- 6 large cans (16 ounce) kidney beans, drained and rinsed
- 6 cups cooked rice (I prefer brown)
- 3 pounds andouille sausage, casings removed
- 3 large chopped onions
- 3 large chopped green peppers
- 2 stalks celery, diced
- 6 large chopped tomatoes
- 1 bulb garlic, peeled and minced
- 2 teaspoons dried oregano
- 2 teaspoons dried parsley
- ¼ cup olive oil
- Hot sauce, salt and pepper to taste

Total time: Approximately one hour
Serves: 25

Step 1:

Warm Dutch oven over medium heat, add oil and bring to smoke point. Add sausage, onions, celery and garlic. Sauté until caramelized. Add spices to taste and tomatoes, heat until hot.

Step 2:

Mix beans with cooked ingredients, mashing down to develop gravy. Bring to a slow simmer for at least 10 minutes. Top with rice, serve warm.

Bedding: 21, 43-44, 78

Beer Bread: 131-132

Breakfast Pudding: 148

Breakfasts: 143-145

Bruschetta: 141-142

Camp Stir Fry: 176-177

Canned Cakes: 180-181

Children: 46-49, 52-53, 88, 93-96

Clothing: 10, 22-25, 112

Clothing Optional: 52-53, 86-87

Crispy Rice Treats: 184

Cucumber Salad: 196

Desserts: 179

Dinners: 163-165

Drumming: 24, 54-55, 59, 79-80

Easy Camp Chili: 172-173

Easy French Toast: 149-150

Etiquette: 51-56

Fee Phi Faux Pho: 197-199

Food Choices/Needs: 53-54

Fool-Proof Artisan Bread: 128-130

Happy Snacky Cracker Platter: 154-155

Holiday-Inspired Dressing: 187-188

Kitchen: 10, 26-33, 63-75, 79

Lettuce Wraps: 158-159

Loaded Deviled Eggs: 189-190

Location, Choosing a: 19, 59-61, 77-81

Lori's Curry: 168-169

Lori's Grilling Sauce: 137-140

Lunches: 151-153

Musical Performances: 100-104

Noise Ordinances: 55-56

Orangy Muffins: 146-147

Packing: 7-35, 43-49, 116-119

Part II – Recipes: 121-201

Pets, Bringing: 46

Photography (etiquette): 53

Piggy Pagans: 52, 68-72

Potlucks: 185-186

Red Beans and Rice: 200-201

Respect: 46-49, 51-56, 83-90

Responsibility: 52, 88-89

Sample Festival Menu: 123-127

Sausages and Kraut: 166-167

Sex/Sexuality: 11-12, 52, 86-90

Shepherd's Pie: 174-175

Smoking (etiquette): 51-52, 106

Southwest Burritos: 193-194

Spicy Guacamole: 195

Stove Top Jam: 133-134

Stuffed Cabbages (Galumpkis) 170-171

Super Chunky Red Sauce: 135-136

Super Easy Trifle: 182-183

Supplies: 15-36

Tent, Choosing a: 15-21

Tent, Decorating a: 77-79

Tuna Pasta Salad: 160-161

Veggie Wraps: 156-157

Vending: 105-115

Watermelon Centerpiece: 191-192

`Work Shifts: 93-100

Workshops: 96-100

A Guide to Pagan Camping

About the Author

Lori Dake is, first and foremost, a dedicated wife, mother and proud Chicago native. She runs an independent record label with her husband and is a classically trained musician and artist. Perhaps in stark contrast to her spiritual beliefs and love of nature, her unconventional interests include extreme heavy metal, sophomoric humor, campy horror films and people watching. Politically, Mrs. Dake is socially liberal to moderate yet fiscally conservative. She reads at least three newspapers each day, and she admires the everyday common folk over polished professionals.

Mrs. Dake founded the Chicago Pagan Parents with other parents within the local community and has hosted several youth-centric events. Currently, her primary focus has been assisting their only child. He is a high-marking homeschool graduate and will be reenlisting with the U.S. Army later this year.

www.ingramcontent.com/pod-product-compliance
Lightning Source LLC
Chambersburg PA
CBHW061639040426
42446CB00010B/1489